The Ten Commitments

Other books by David Simon

The Wisdom of Healing

Return to Wholeness

Vital Energy

The Chopra Center Herbal Handbook
(with coauthor Deepak Chopra)

Grow Younger, Live Longer
(with coauthor Deepak Chopra)

Magical Beginnings, Enchanted Lives
(with coauthors Deepak Chopra and Vicki Abrams)

The Seven Spiritual Laws of Yoga
(with coauthor Deepak Chopra)

THE TEN
COMMITMENTS
Translating Good Intentions into Great Choices

DAVID SIMON, M.D.

Foreword by Deepak Chopra

Health Communications, Inc.
Deerfield Beach, Florida

www.bcibooks.com

Bible references from *The Pentateuch and Hoftorahs,* edited by Dr. J. H. Hert, C.H. Soncino Press, London 5449-1988.

Library of Congress Cataloging-in-Publication Data
is available from the Library of Congress.

Publisher: Health Communications, Inc.
          3201 S.W. 15th Street
          Deerfield Beach, FL 33442-8190

Cover design by Larissa Hise Henoch
Inside book design by Dawn Von Strolley Grove

*This book is dedicated to my fellow seekers who have
Tolerance as their practice,
Nature as their house of worship,
and
A God that answers to all names or none.*

TABLE OF CONTENTS

ACKNOWLEDGMENTS

Each step toward the manifestation of this book was supported by many loving souls. In particular, I wish to express my heartfelt gratitude to:

My literary agent, Lynn Franklin, for her unwavering support and relentless efforts to bring this work to fruition;

My editor, Bret Witter, for his commitment to make this book accessible to the widest possible audience;

Daniel Ladinsky, for his amazing talent in bringing Hafiz to life and for generously allowing me to share him;

My beloved family, Pam, Max, Sara and Isabel Simon, for their unconditional love and acceptance of my divinity and humanity;

My parents, Myron and Lee Shirley, for lovingly imprinting upon me the power of commitment through their words and actions;

Deepak Chopra, for the unending inspiration and insights he shares with me;

Charley Paz, Ray Chambers, Jose Busquets and Howard

Simon for serving as the living cornerstones of the Chopra Center; and

My dedicated Chopra Center staff, who demonstrate on a daily basis their commitment to helping people find peace, well-being, love and purpose in their lives:

David Greenspan, Max Simon, Asha MacIsaac, Anastacia Leigh, Teresa Long, Lorri Gifford, Patty Schmucker, Kristy Reeves, Neal Tricarico, Samara Tricarico, Claire Diab, Grace Wilson, Michela Baca, Brent Becvar, Monica Campos, Jennifer Childe, Lindsay Clark, Jay DeGuzman, Erika DeSimone, Alex Dial, Nancy Ede, Kana Emily-Mazza, Monica Ensign, Leili Farhangi, Alisa Feldman, Mel Finnerty, Jenifer Fitting, Kelly Flaherty, Carissa Garrard, Vanessa Gibbs, Tim Herr, Emily Hobgood, Amanda Ishimaru, Jennifer Johnson, James Knight, Joe Lancaster, Kendal Manning, Alisha McShane, Brooke Myers, Carolyn Rangel, Felicia Rangel, Julian Romero, Jill Romnes, Mollie Shea, Danielle Signorelli, Julie Strassburger, Alexis Ufland, Michelle Whitmer and Angela Wiskirken.

Permission to use translations of Hafiz poetry was graciously provided by Daniel Ladinsky. Complete poems are published in:
I Heard God Laughing, Paris Printing, 2004, Pont Richmond, CA;
The Gift, Penguin Compass, 1999, NY, NY;
The Subject Tonight is Love, Penguin Compass, 2003, NY, NY.

FOREWORD

Commitment is Intention

Commitment is one-pointed intention toward the fulfillment of your deepest desires. Commitment initiated at a deep level of awareness orchestrates its own fulfillment. The organization of nature's forces to fulfill your intentions occurs as the result of a shift in context and meaning. When you recognize that reality is a selective act of attention and interpretation—a selective act of perception—you become capable of consciously cocreating your life. Like a newborn infant who emerges from the womb, intentions that carry the power of commitment never return to their unmanifest state.

Commitment is the ultimate assertion of human freedom. It enables you to take quantum leaps in creativity, which opens the possibility for new dimensions of awareness. Commitment provides the technology that allows you to break the habits that confine you in the prison of conditioning. Through the power of commitment, your personal intentions engage the forces of nature so that fulfillment becomes your daily reality. Knowing that your intentions

will be spontaneously fulfilled enables you to live a life of freedom, creativity and joy, without anxiety or strain.

I am pleased and honored to introduce this beautiful and enlightening book, *The Ten Commitments*, written by my dear friend and colleague, David Simon. As partners and co-founders of the Chopra Center, David and I have collaborated for more than a decade. Through our shared vision we have developed seminars and programs on mind/body health and spirituality, and we have coauthored five books.

Most of our work together has been dedicated to translating ancient Eastern wisdom into the language of modern science. We have been enthusiastic in our quest to show how the perennial wisdom of Vedic philosophy offers timeless solutions to the challenges of modern life. We have seen the value of this integrative approach in the lives of the thousands of people who participate each year in Chopra Center workshops and programs.

In this fascinating and uniquely insightful book, David explores the core tenets of Western spiritual values. He demonstrates how, with a subtle yet powerful shift in perception, the essential truths of East and West merge to create a compelling vision for a better world.

Truth is that which transcends time and space. In *The Ten Commitments*, David explores the truths of Western society and translates them into a modern vocabulary that transcends their Western origins. Just as he has helped make the essential message of Ayurveda, the 5,000-year-old healing

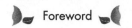

system of India, accessible to people around the world, he has now shone his light on ancient Western truths to bring us a new understanding that has profound and universal implications.

Our beautiful yet delicate planet is at a crossroads. We can either continue to relate to each other with a tribal mentality in which we emphasize the distinctions between us, or we can pierce the mask of duality and embrace our underlying unity. The first choice inevitably leads to conflict, xenophobia and ecological devastation. The second holds the promise for peace, compassion, and the honoring of our interconnectedness with the web of life.

I am grateful that David has simply and eloquently elaborated a compelling yet practical path to restore wholeness to our lives, both individually and collectively. I encourage you to implement *The Ten Commitments* in your life and consciously share in our quest to heal and transform the world.

Deepak Chopra, May 2005

The Ten Commandments

*I am the Lord, thy God, who brought you
out of the house of slavery.
Thou shalt not make unto thee a graven image.
Thou shalt not take the name
of the Lord thy God in vain.
Remember the Sabbath day to keep it holy.
Honor thy father and thy mother.
Thou shalt not kill.
Thou shalt not commit adultery.
Thou shalt not steal.
Thou shalt not bear false witness
against thy neighbor.
Thou shalt not covet.*

The Ten Commitments

I commit to freedom.

I commit to authenticity.

I commit to acceptance.

I commit to relax.

I commit to wholeness.

I commit to forgiveness.

I commit to love.

I commit to abundance.

I commit to truth.

I commit to peace.

TRANSLATING INTENTIONS INTO CHOICES

When all your desires are distilled
You will cast just two votes:
To love more, And be happy.
Hafiz

You are reading these words because there is something in your life you would like to change. It may be something you want to relinquish but are afraid to let go. It may be something you are longing for but have been unable to manifest. We're here together to help translate your intentions into choices. This requires the power of commitment.

Commitment is a contract between your body, mind and soul. Your body has needs. Your mind has desires. Beyond the immediacy of your physical cravings and your emotional longings is your soul, encouraging you to make the choices that are most likely to bring enduring peace of mind. It is whispering these words to you: "I want you to be happy," "I want you to be healthy," "I want you to have love," "I want you to live a life of meaning and purpose." It may be difficult to hear these life-celebrating messages from the depths of your being if your mind is turbulent and your body is in distress.

Although it is usually taken for granted that people know what the words "body, mind and soul" mean, I'd like to offer my definitions, which I'll be using throughout the book. Your *body* is the collection of molecules that enables you to experience the world. It includes the sensory equipment that connects you to your environment (hearing, feeling, seeing, tasting and smelling) and the motor systems that enable you to act upon the world (your vocal apparatus, hands and feet). Each day you metabolize sensory experiences through the ever-changing chemistry and electricity of your nervous system, which in turn influences every cell and organ in your body. Through this process, your experiences become your biology.

Your *mind* is a field of thoughts, engaging in a continuous conversation about what has happened, what is happening and what might happen to you. In response to your perpetual experiences, you make discriminations, evaluations and judgments, colored by emotional reactions. Your thoughts, memories, desires and feelings are various expressions of your mind.

Your *soul* is the silent witness to your mind and body. Your body is changing—you only need look at a photograph from a decade ago to see that your body today is different from what it was in the past. Your mind is changing—your beliefs about yourself and the world are different now compared to earlier times in your life. Underlying this dimension of change is your quietly observing soul, providing continuity to your identity. When your observing soul, thought-generating mind and physical body are aligned, you are most likely to translate your intentions into choices that result in the desired outcome.

Commitment implies action. When you make a commitment, you dedicate yourself to a course of action that you believe will result in the expansion of happiness and well-being. The fulfillment of a commitment is realized when your intentions become your automatic style of functioning in the world. If you make a commitment to enhance your physical fitness, your commitment yields its fruits when you find yourself looking forward to your exercise time or your healthy meal. The fulfillment of your commitment to stop smoking manifests when you lose the desire to light a cigarette. Commitment means moving through a door of change through which you do not intend to return.

The Challenge of Commitment

Responsible parents devote much of their child-rearing energy to setting boundaries. As soon as children are capable of making choices, parents begin the eighteen-plus-year process of instilling commandments intended to keep them safe and functional in society. "Do this . . . don't do that . . ." are the developmental tools applied to shape our outer boundaries, defining what is and is not appropriate and acceptable.

In response to the imposition of external limits, children struggle to set internal boundaries, which appears as resistance to being told what to do. By about two years of age children learn to assert their independence through use of the powerful word "No!" Practiced relentlessly, the talent for resisting authority is honed during teenage years. The process of maturing into adulthood requires, in large part, the development of skills to camouflage resistance to parents, teachers, bosses, doctors, clergy, policemen and other authority figures whose approval or support we need. Authority figures may change, proscriptions may change, but the deep desire to control our own lives remains.

Since tribal times, societal elders have attempted to reinforce rules by enlisting the power of the gods. If the human complications of lying, cheating or stealing are not enough to discourage you, the fear of divine wrath may be persuasive. If the likelihood of causing pain among family members is inadequate to avoid adultery, then the possibility of basting in hell may convince you. Moral codes are designed to protect individuals and communities from unnecessary suffering; nevertheless, reinforcing demands with fear is as likely to provoke resistance as it does to invoke acquiescence.

The Ten Commandments are the moral guideposts of our Judeo-Christian society. As the underlying precepts of order in our Western world, they have guided our ethical choices for millennia. They offer a powerful prescription for moral health, and if being told how to behave resulted in people doing what was ultimately good for them, the world would be a much better place. Unfortunately, it is one thing to be commanded; it is another to make conscious choices that serve the greatest good.

We are commanded not to kill, but over sixteen thousand

people are murdered each year in the United States, and in the name of God or country, tens of thousands are killed in armed conflicts. We are commanded not to steal, but over ten million thefts occur annually. We have a prohibition against adultery, yet studies suggest that at least half of married people engage in extramarital affairs. Treated as children, people respond as children. It is time to replace commandment with commitment.

What You Think, You Become

Your parents were writing the opening lines to the screenplay of your life by the time you arrived onstage, and for much of your existence you have been reading from the script you were handed. If your story is unfolding as you hoped it would as a child, you have probably intuitively implemented the principles of this book. You are among the fortunate ones who have learned to commit consciously to your dreams until they manifest. If, however, deep in your soul, you suspect that you have not yet realized your full potential and are worthy of more, then this book is for you. *The Ten Commitments* is for people willing to become the change they want to see. It is for those who can embrace the idea that free will is the greatest gift to humanity, and that despite what has happened up until now, we are capable of writing a better next chapter. Albert Einstein defined insanity as "doing the same thing over and over again and expecting different results." *The Ten Commitments* is offered as a guide to sanity.

As a doctor, I have been privileged to hear the challenges and intimate problems of my patients for more than three decades. Distress takes many different forms. For one person, it may be attacks of anxiety or bouts of depression. For another, it may be unrelenting pain or fatigue. Acute or chronic life overload may manifest as a host of physical concerns, including insomnia, digestive problems or immunological vulnerability. Weight problems, eating disorders, migraines and high blood pressure are often expressions of underlying inner turbulence. Regardless of the stated reason a person comes to a doctor, there is inevitably a core experience of discomfort—either physical or emotional. People are in pain and want to get out of it. I often find myself asking the same question of my patients: *"Are you willing to do things differently in order to have a different outcome?"*

Release Your Past

There is value in understanding how you arrived at your present situation. Chronic emotional and physical health concerns can reflect early discord. Seeing the connection may be beneficial, as long as you do not add insult to injury by taking on too much responsibility for a condition that has other important factors outside your control. Knowing your father was ill-tempered may help gain insight into your irritable bowel syndrome. Acknowledging that your mother was emotionally remote may help you understand your eating disorder or anxiety attacks. Honestly looking at your past can be helpful in appreciating the current condition in which you find yourself. At times, it can even be liberating.

However, life is short, and spending years trying to "get to the bottom of the problem" may not be the most successful strategy. It is possible to understand clearly why you are unhappy, but still not be any happier. It is possible to know why you have made bad choices in the past, but this knowledge may not enable you to make better ones now. The most important principle of healing and transformation is: *For our lives to change, we have to change.*

There is a skill in charting the course of your life that requires finesse and timing. Seeing the bigger picture and making more conscious choices is a path of power and subtlety. It requires clarity of purpose and purity of intention. It requires commitment.

Unlearning

Although human beings have the capacity to make choices, most people live their lives as conditioned as Pavlovian dogs, reacting in predictable ways to the situations, circumstances and people they encounter. Because there is security in doing things the same way over and over, people stay in relationships that do not nourish them, hold on to jobs that provide limited outlet for their creativity and maintain daily routines that numb them to the miracles unfolding around them in every moment of life.

Admit it. You are a creature of habit. You awaken at about the same time every day, use the same toothpaste and eat the same breakfast. You drive to work along the same route, listen to the same radio stations and arrive at the office at about the same time. When you get home you watch the same television shows, go through the same evening ablutions and get to bed at about the same time. A private investigator keeping track of your patterns for a week could predict where you would be at a given time on a given day with a high degree of accuracy. This is the conditioned human experience.

There is no reason to change your patterns if you are getting what you need out of life. But if you recognize the need to release inhibiting habits in pursuit of greater happiness, love, well-being and meaning in your life, commitment is the proven path.

The premise of a commandment is that without threat, direct or implied, a desired behavior will not occur, as in, "If you don't clean up your room, you're not going to the party!" Children's behavior may be temporarily controlled through commandments. Genuine and enduring healing and transformation in adults can only occur through commitment.

I recently spoke on the Ten Commitments to a group that included members of the clergy. A few protested when I suggested that the Ten Commandments were insufficient.

They asserted that the "masses" need to be treated like children and that the Ten Commandments have successfully kept people in line for millennia. I could not confidently disagree with their interpretation of past collective needs, but I am convinced that for humanity to survive and thrive, we must assume personal responsibility for our choices. It is my hope that this new language for our old precepts will create a new reality.

Commitment Versus Affirmation

Repeatedly affirming something seldom leads to lasting change. Successful people do not continuously tell themselves, "I am a powerful person." Physically fit people do not perpetually remind themselves, "I can control my eating." Emotionally secure people do not constantly affirm, "I am a confident person." Lasting benefits rarely result from affirmations alone. Benefits derive from behaviors; behaviors derive from commitment. What do you want? Are you prepared to take the steps to get it?

In *The Ten Commitments* we will explore how to make good choices, not out of fear of being caught or punished, but because they reflect the person you really want to be—the sacred being you sense you are. As a result, the quiet voice of your soul that wants you to be happy, know love, feel vital, and have meaning and purpose in life will find its expression.

THE FIRST COMMITMENT:

I COMMIT TO FREEDOM

I am the Lord, thy God, who brought you
out of the house of slavery.
Exodus 20:2

We have not come here to take prisoners,
But to surrender ever more deeply
To freedom and joy.
Hafiz

Most people live in voluntary confinement, believing that the security they gain outweighs the freedom surrendered. But the desire for freedom is not relinquished so easily. Freedom to speak, to act, to love and to find meaning in life are universal impulses expressed across time and culture. The first of the Ten Commandments proclaims that God freed his people from slavery. This is the essential message of spirituality—freedom from internally or externally imposed limitations—freedom from bondage.

The aspiration for self-determination is a basic human impulse. Whether considering political or personal independence, true liberation calls you to free yourself from limiting ideas and habitual behaviors. When you live within constricted views of yourself, you suffocate your creativity, enthusiasm and joy. When you move beyond your limitations and expand your sense of identity, exhilaration rises from your depths.

Internal Liberation

Genuine inner freedom is the ultimate aim of life. It is the unspoken goal of every thought you have and action you take. In the Eastern wisdom traditions, freedom from self-imposed limitations goes by many names: *nirvana, moksha, enlightenment.* This state of internal liberation is transcendent to external situations and circumstances. It is freedom from conditioning, freedom from the past and freedom from the predictable. The opportunity to achieve this level of freedom distinguishes human beings from other sentient animals, although few people unwrap this sacred gift received at birth.

Most people mistakenly believe that external forces limit their happiness. "I am depressed because I'm stuck in an abusive marriage." "I have this ulcer because my boss is controlling." "My relationships repeatedly fail because my father abandoned me when I was young." We accept these limiting beliefs and engage in perpetual internal negotiations with these restrictive voices, never reaching agreement on the terms for our release. Common excuses I hear include: "As soon as my youngest child graduates high school, I'm leaving this toxic marriage," or "Once I'm vested in my pension plan, I am saying good-bye to this stagnant job," or "After I get through the holidays, I am going to start exercising." It's time to use the key residing in your soul to unlock the door that frees you from self-imposed incarceration.

Open the door to freedom. Commit to relinquishing conditioned reactions and energy-squandering behaviors. Listen to your inner mind and identify where you are living in bondage. Try it now.

Take a few deep breaths, close your eyes and become aware of any sensations of discomfort in your body. If you identify a place in your body that feels constricted or congested, ask yourself, "What life issue is this sensation telling me about?" Recognizing that emotional conflicts are often expressed as physical tension, allow any bodily sensations to bring your attention to possible mental debates you are having with yourself. Ask what you can do to create inner peace and free yourself from conflict. Plot your escape.

Overcoming Limits

Our favorite fairy tales and epic sagas are the stories of heroic characters overcoming obstacles to freedom. Internally imposed limitations are embodied as the troll hiding under the bridge, the monster guarding the entrance to the cave, the wicked witch in the gingerbread house and the wolf in the woods. These adversaries live within us.

Tales that celebrate heroes and heroines who vanquish the demons attempting to steal their love, their innocence, their treasure or their lives remind us of our power to overcome obstacles. From Hansel and Gretel to Spiderman, stories about freedom's triumph over bondage inspire our heart and soul.

Being fully alive means continually striving to expand freedom in our lives. When diminished, it is usually surrendered incrementally. A baby elephant tied to a stake is conditioned to believe it cannot move about freely. Years later when the elephant has the strength to pull a tree from the ground, it remains confined by a rope around its leg. Most of us have been taught to stay close to our stakes. It is time to cut the cord of bondage.

The Sense of "I"

We are born into bodies that have innate protective mechanisms. When we are thirsty, we seek fluids. When we are hungry, we seek food. When we are tired, we sleep. When we feel threatened we have the spontaneous impulse to run or fight. The body's needs are relatively simple and oriented to the present moment. If we have just eaten a meal, our body doesn't agonize over what to do when it becomes hungry tomorrow.

The mind on the other hand has the remarkable capacity to torture us with ruminations about experiences from the past and worry about needs and threats far into the future. Mental anguish often comes from bondage—the belief that we are living in circumstances from which we have no possibility of freeing ourselves.

Being a person means having a body, a mind and a point of reference. With incarnation comes the sense of "I." Coincident with the dawning of the sense of "I" is awareness that there is "not I." In comparison, the "not I" seems a lot bigger than the "I." This recognition of our vulnerability and dependency generates anxiety. We then spend our lives striving to relieve anxiety by enhancing our sense of "I" with acquisitions and accomplishments, creating a self-image through our possessions, positions and beliefs.

The self-image or ego is what we hold to be true about ourselves and what we want others to believe about us. Most people believe they are their self-image and, therefore, diligently strive to protect it. In the defense of our image, we imprison our spirit.

Our egos develop by identifying with things external to ourselves. For the first several months of life we are barely aware that anything exists outside of us. Our entire awareness is body centered; comfort and discomfort are consequences of whether or not our basic needs are fulfilled. If we are hungry and mother's milk is immediately available we feel content. If we are tired and are put into our crib, we feel relieved. Whenever there is a delay between the arising of a need and its fulfillment, we experience discomfort, which we demonstrate by an ear-piercing wail. Nature has designed the sound of a howling infant to incite caregivers to do whatever is necessary to stop the noise, be it day or night.

Eventually, it dawns on young humans that something exists other than themselves. We learn to call this first other *mother*, but even before we develop language, we begin honing our need-meeting skills to avoid discomfort and anxiety. We learn to seduce, entice and amuse. We become skilled at imitation, intimidation, manipulation and coercion. We develop our ability to appease, entertain and amuse. We create a personality.

As we gain autonomy, we envelop our vulnerable selves with attachments. The ego begins asserting ownership over people and things. "This is my toy . . . my mom . . . my cookie . . . my turn." When our sense of ownership is affirmed, our anxiety is reduced, but when our sense of control is threatened our anxiety escalates.

By the time we are adults, we have woven a protective shroud that declares to the world who we believe we are. Our hairstyle, clothing, cars, dwellings, jobs, friends and the way we take our coffee all define the image we have crafted. We then invest considerable emotional energy in the protection of our self-image. When the postal clerk treats us curtly, we feel irritated because he has offended our self-image. When someone fails to compliment our new hairstyle, we are annoyed because we have not received the anticipated return on the investment in our self-image. When another driver refuses to let us in on the highway, we feel aggravated because our self-image has been bruised.

Defending the Indefensible

The problem with investing so much in defending our self-image is that, simply stated, it isn't real. Although human beings spend incalculable amounts of energy shoring up their egos, there is no real substance to one's self-image. Therefore, no matter how polished people look from the outside, they cannot feel completely secure because at some level they know that the image they have crafted is not real. Their inner freedom is limited by their need for approval and control.

These needs are not wrong or bad; they are just limiting. Our motivation for personal enhancement benefits both individuals and society. Discontent is the basis of our perpetual striving to improve, and it is often feelings of inadequacy that compel us to accomplish and achieve. And yet we will never find genuine peace or realize freedom as a result of our achievements. With each accomplishment we experience a temporary wave of satisfaction followed immediately by a new desire. This is the nature of life—a desire spurs us into action, which leaves an impression that gives rise to a new desire.

The lingering discontent we feel despite our successes incites the voices that disturb our peace. The voice that promises contentment through the future acquisition of a thing, position or relationship keeps us in bondage by playing on our insecurities. Genuine freedom can only blossom when this inner voice is quieted.

Self-Importance, Self-Pity

Self-importance and insecurity are two sides of the same coin. It is one of life's paradoxes that these apparently opposing qualities are so intimately linked. People who wield power indiscriminately are usually driven by deep insecurities about their own value.

On the other hand, insecurity often derives from an inflated sense of importance. Although Copernicus announced almost five hundred years ago that we are not the center of the universe, the human ego has not yet accepted the truth of this information. From the perspective of our self-image, everything revolves around us.

When a teenage girl becomes anxious about going to a party because she has a pimple on her chin, she imagines that everyone she encounters will be focusing on her minute blemish. An otherwise straight-A student who agonizes over receiving a B on a calculus test imagines that this evidence of imperfection will be the hot topic of conversation among his peers. Embarrassment and shame emerge from the inner dialogue of self-importance.

Freedom from Conditioned Responses

Opportunities to be liberated from our constricted sense of self present themselves on a daily basis. We simply need to pay attention to the external experiences that trigger our need to defend our self-image. Try the following simple exercise.

1. Identify a Violation

Identify the most recent time you were upset, preferably within the last twenty-four to forty-eight hours. It could be a minor annoying incident with a retail clerk or a more distressing encounter with an intimate friend or family member.

2. Get Clear on the Details

Recall the experience in as much detail as you can remember. Close your eyes and evoke the sounds and images that provoked you.

3. Acknowledge the Sensations

Identify and describe the emotions that arise as you consider this encounter. Listen attentively to the signals your body is sending, relinquishing the need to judge them. Feel the sensations while observing the inner dialogue to which it is connected.

4. Recognize the Trespass

You experienced a triggering of your feelings because something happened that was inconsistent with what you want to believe is true about you. See if you can recognize the upsetting encounter as a violation of your self-image.

5. Reclaim Your Sanity

Envision how you could have responded in a way that would be less reactive and therefore more empowering.

The Everyday Pursuit of Freedom

My recent experience with a patient demonstrates how this simple five-step process can be liberating. An accomplished and successful man, George was experiencing considerable distress as a result of being stuck in a long-standing emotional pattern.

"This guy at work is driving me crazy!" George complained to me. "He's manipulative, power hungry and a real brownnoser. I'm a nonviolent person, but I have been having fantasies of breaking the windows of his BMW."

After a year as a financial consultant at a major brokerage house, George had a growing clientele and was rising quickly in his organization. When Alex, a financial planner from another office, was transferred to the desk next to his, he immediately sensed unwanted competition. George found himself spending an increasing amount of time being annoyed and distracted by his new associate. Both during and after work hours, George was engaged in a combative inner conversation. Alex had roused George's anxiety tyrant.

George agreed to work through this process with me, which unfolded in the following manner:

1. Identification of the Violation

George identified an episode earlier that day in which he had overheard the managing director complimenting Alex on his acquisition of a new account.

2. Clarification of Details

When asked to get clear on the details, George initially ranted about how Alex was "sucking up" to the director, but admitted that all he actually heard was Alex saying he had received confirmation that assets were being transferred to their branch, to which the director responded, "Good work."

3. Sensation Acknowledgment

When asked to elaborate his feelings (acknowledging the sensations), George initially came up with a series of judgments: "I feel he is dishonest and greedy and trying to sabotage me. I feel he is receiving special treatment." I encouraged him to move from his mind to his body and describe the emotions driving his thoughts. He recognized that feelings of anxiety, insecurity and fear of failure were just below the surface.

4. Trespass Recognition

Identifying the alleged trespass, George saw that his perception of himself as top dog was violated. His self-image as the fastest rising superstar was challenged by Alex's successes.

5. Sanity Reclamation

Recognizing that his own accomplishments were independent of Alex's, George was able to reclaim his sanity by shifting his perspective in relationship to his colleague. George saw that indulging in his well-honed anxiety response increased rather than diminished his chances of failing. He made the commitment to focus on serving his clients' needs while becoming free from his compulsion to compare himself constantly with others.

Choose Consciously

Consider this scenario. For the third time in as many weeks, you are late to a manager's meeting. One of your coworkers chides you for your recurrent tardiness and you feel offended. You respond by denying that this is characteristic of you and elaborate all the important responsibilities you were attending to on behalf of the company that resulted in your late arrival today. You then go on the offensive highlighting other meetings in which you were the first person to arrive and your accuser was late. Your insecurity and self-importance are aroused, and your inner dialogue sounds like the following:

Who does she think she is? I don't need her telling me how to do my job. I'm working twelve-hour days for this company, but people only comment when they find something wrong. From now on I'm no longer going the extra mile.

Although it may not seem like it at the time, encounters like this are opportunities for freedom. Knowing that efforts to protect your self-image are usually a waste of energy, you are free to consider creative solutions.

When someone points out something about which you feel vulnerable, you have three choices. You can defend yourself, you can rationalize, or you can explore if the characteristic you are denying or defending may benefit from some attention.

In the example above you could attack the other person, you could rationalize that you deserve to be late considering how much is always on your plate, or you could acknowledge the unsolicited information about your tardiness and use it to make a commitment to create more breathing room between your tasks. Rather than indulging in the process of being offended, empower yourself by using the information to either change or accept. Exercising choice, you move from bondage into freedom.

Commit to Freedom

Change is the only constant in life. It is the one thing we can count on. Most human suffering comes from resisting change.

We either resist new things from entering or familiar things from leaving, and in this resistance we struggle. Resisting the inevitable, we become entrapped in our limited ideas of how things should be. Genuine peace is not dependent upon things being a certain way, because inevitably they will change and peace will be disturbed.

From a spiritual perspective, freedom from attachment to a particular outcome is the ultimate expression of liberation. We can choose the actions we take, but we cannot control the consequences of our choices. Freedom is expanded by focusing our energies on the options available and making choices that have the greatest chance of increasing peace and happiness in our lives.

After liberation from Egypt, the Israelites wandered in the desert for forty years. This reminds us that after taking a step toward freedom, it may take some time for the full expression of the choice to manifest (although hopefully not forty years). Entering into the land of milk and honey is possible only after you make the commitment to freedom. Part the sea.

I demonstrate my commitment to freedom by:

1) Paying attention to my body and the sensations it generates to identify and quiet internal conflicts.

2) Cultivating the habit of asking myself, "What choice can I make *now* to move in the direction of well-being?"

3) Taking an honest inventory of my internal restrictions that fail to serve me and changing one thing that will expand my freedom.

THE SECOND COMMITMENT:
I COMMIT TO AUTHENTICITY

Thou shalt not make unto thee a graven image.
Exodus 20:4

God disguised as myriad things
And playing a game of tag
Has kissed you and said,
"You're it—I mean you're Really IT!"
Hafiz

Your striving for acceptance and approval began before you can remember. As a child, you quickly learned that how you behaved, looked, spoke and even thought determined whether it would be easy or challenging for you to meet your needs. You learned to adapt to and align with the values of others in order to receive the attention and nurturing you needed. The second commitment encourages you to look consciously at the masks you've donned and remove those that inhibit the expression of your authentic self.

Authenticity is an alignment between your beliefs, your desires and your choices in the world. Desires change throughout the course of a life, but agreement between ideals, aspirations and deeds is key to a life of peace, happiness and success. When you act in ways unlikely to fulfill your genuine desires, you experience the inner friction of a life out of alignment. Desires that are in alignment with core beliefs generate powerful actions. Like a wave that draws from the depths of the ocean, actions connected to your authentic self are more likely to manifest your intentions.

Desires boil down to a few basic categories. We have desires for material abundance, for nurturing love, for meaningful work and for connection to the deep mystery of life. Choices that are in alignment with what we know, feel and believe to be true generate a natural sense of ease and confidence. When we allow distractions to intervene between our core values and the choices we make in the world, our energy is depleted. These distractions become false idols that block access to the divine.

The word "authenticity" is derived from the Latin *authenticus,* meaning coming from the real author. Being authentic means assuming the responsibility for writing the story of your life. Many people find themselves playing a character in their real-life drama, but do not recall consciously auditioning for the role.

Jenna's parents divorced when she was four years of age, and within a year, her mother remarried. A year later, this family broke apart and her mother moved back with Jenna to her hometown so they could be near her parents. Jenna lived with her mother and grandparents until she graduated high school. Shortly after moving out, Jenna took a job as a waitress and promptly began drinking, using cocaine and engaging in casual sex. Six months later she became pregnant. Her boyfriend stayed around until a month after the baby was born and then disappeared from their lives.

A year later she became pregnant again and this time decided to marry the father. Three years later they remain together, but their relationship is shaky. Jenna complains of constant fatigue and depression.

What would it mean for this woman to be authentic? In serving her false idols of drinking, drugs and casual sex, she traded longer-term pain for momentary relief. Making decisions most of her life on the basis of what provided immediate relief from her emotional and physical pain, Jenna had only recently begun to consciously consider how she could find authentic identity, meaning and purpose in life.

Each of us is engaged in a similar pursuit. As interdependent beings, we borrow the beliefs and perspectives of those with whom we associate. There is inherent tension between our need for approval and our need to express our authentic selves in the world. We try on different disguises in the hope that one will fit, resulting in the love and acceptance we seek.

We have many facets to our nature. We have light and dark, deep and superficial, expansive and restrictive sides. Authenticity requires that we embrace our complexity while consciously expressing those characteristics that align with our intentions. We become the choices we make, but are often not conscious we are making choices. Becoming a conscious choice-maker translates into greater authenticity.

Authentic Choice Making

Committing to authenticity means taking responsibility for what you choose to do and what you choose not to do.

Health and vitality require reducing ingestion of experiences and substances that leave a negative residue in the mind and body, while maximizing ingestion of experiences and substances that generate a nourishing influence.

Human beings develop habits easily, and almost everyone can become addicted. You know you're addicted to something when its withdrawal causes you to experience emotional or physical discomfort. There are, of course, a host of potent addictive chemicals, like alcohol, illegal drugs, pain pills and psychoactive medications. There are also the more subtly addictive substances, such as caffeine, chocolate and sugar. Addictive behaviors, such as gambling, shopping or risk taking, can also trap people in life-damaging patterns. People can be addicted to the status symbols of money, power or prestige. I meet many people addicted to achievement, approval, perfection and control. I see people addicted to arguing, exaggeration or lying. Addiction to work often feeds other addictions.

The quest for authenticity requires you to look honestly at your habits and patterns and determine if they are serving you well or not. Regardless of whether or not it ultimately serves a higher purpose, every addictive or habitual behavior serves the immediate goal of reducing anxiety. Since the work of upholding your self-image is so demanding, anything you can do to reduce tension may be temporarily attractive. If the behavior is successful at momentarily relieving distress, it is easy to become attached to the experience.

Clearing the Obstacles to Authenticity

The challenge facing anyone striving for personal transformation is how to translate their good intentions into good choices. Well-meaning people with good intentions to heal and transform their lives often find the walls of their rut too steep to surmount on their own. Moving from *wanting to change* into *actually changing* is difficult. It requires identifying negative patterns, releasing them and replacing them with positive ones.

It is not easy to break a habit for two main reasons. The first is that the habit, at least originally, fulfills a need. The second is that neural circuits become established in the brain, reinforcing the predictable pattern of behavior. Habits generate biochemical and physiological changes that perpetuate behaviors. All habits have emotional and physical components, and both must be addressed if you are to change a habit from one that is life-damaging to one that is life-promoting.

Step One: Identify the Obstacle

A habit must be acknowledged in order to be changed. The idea, "I can stop this behavior anytime I want," is most often an expression of denial. A habit or addiction is something that produces discomfort upon its withdrawal, which is part of the reason people continue engaging in the behavior. An unwanted habit cannot be relinquished unless it is brought into conscious awareness.

Take a few moments to identify a habit that is interfering with your health and happiness. Close your eyes and ask yourself, "What do I really want to change? What do I really need to change?" Facing your adversary directly reduces the likelihood that it will sabotage you from the dark corners of your psyche.

Step Two: Present Moment Behavior

Bring your full attention into your habit. If you pick your lip, be completely conscious of the behavior. If you smoke cigarettes, bring your complete attention to the act of smoking. If you drink vodka, gamble or argue with your spouse, witness your behavior. Smoking while on the phone, listening to the television while balancing the checkbook or engaging in an argument while driving the car prevents you from being aware of the pattern because your mind is divided. Stop whatever else you are doing along with the habitual behavior and connect with your inner observer.

If possible, *put down this book and engage in your habit now.* Bite your nails, smoke a cigarette, pour yourself a glass of wine, get some cookies from the pantry, start an argument with your spouse. Perform your usually unconscious behavior consciously. Move into a mindful mode, slowing down your actions so you can shift from a conditioned to an unconditioned state. Notice the sensations in your body and the thoughts in your mind as you perform this ritual. Shift your internal reference from the doer of the action to the observer. Simply witness your choice without judgments. Practice this.

Step Three: Envision the New

Neural networks in your brain govern your mind and body. When you shift into a witnessing mode and are able to consciously observe your mental and physical habits, you increase your chances of making different choices that can be reinforced through new brain connections.

Close your eyes, take a deep breath and envision the change you would like to see in your life. If you are trying to eat healthier, create a scenario in your mind's eye that includes all the essential components. Envision clearing out junk food from your pantry. Imagine purchasing healthy foods from the market and preparing them in your kitchen. Visualize the health-promoting restaurants where you will eat your lunches. Picture the healthy snacks you will consume in the evening.

If you believe you would benefit from eliminating the half-bottle of wine you've been drinking each evening, imagine how your life will be, absent the alcohol. If you feel it's time to give up arguing and deepen intimacy with your spouse, imagine what this new relationship could be like.

Create the new script in your mind, and then write it down. Read it each day, making revisions that improve the story. When you are clear on what you want, begin the rehearsals.

Step Four: Clear the Space

Set a date and time that you will end the habitual behavior that has become your false idol. Begin by removing temptations from your environment and asking for support from the people in your life. If you want to stop eating sugar, throw out all cookies, candy and cake. If you want to stop smoking pot, eliminate your stashes. If you want to stop drinking beer, clear it out of your house.

Although it may seem that you can handle only one change at a time, my experience is that people who immerse themselves in a total process of healing and transformation are more easily able to eliminate imprisoning habits.

It is generally best to break a habit on Saturday morning, so you have the weekend to focus on the changes you intend to make. For the first seventy-two hours, simplify your life as much as possible. Here are a few suggestions I've found to be helpful.

- Drink plenty of gingerroot herbal tea, a long-standing natural detoxifier. Place a teaspoon of fresh grated ginger in a pint of hot water and sip it throughout the day. Gingerroot tea can be particularly helpful if you are trying to release your attachment to coffee, junk food, cigarettes or alcohol.
- Engage your senses in healthy pleasures while you are releasing. Get a massage, take a yoga class or go for a hike in a beautiful environment.

- Declare the weekend one of global detoxification. Wash your car, clean out your drawers, go through your closet and gather up old clothing to give away. Make as many detoxifying changes in your life as possible.
- Make a schedule of your day's activities in advance. A habit-releasing day may look like the following:

7:00	Wake up without an alarm clock by leaving the curtains partially open.
7:30	Spend time relaxing or meditating to quiet your thoughts.
8:00	Eat a healthy breakfast.
9:00	Take an exercise or yoga class.
11:00	Walk for forty-five minutes.
12:30	Meet a friend for a healthy lunch.
2:00	Plant new flowers in your garden or on your window sill.
5:00	Spend time relaxing or meditating to quiet your thoughts.
6:30	Eat a light dinner.
7:30	Go to movie with a friend/partner.
9:00	Take a warm bath, drink some soothing herbal tea, read a mind-calming book.
10:00	Be in bed with the lights out.

Disengaging from habits requires focused attention and intention. Whether you are withdrawing from a toxic relationship, a toxic job or a toxic substance, the first three days are usually the most challenging. Eliminate your usual distractions so you can stay focused on eliminating the unwanted habit. It starts to get easier if you can remain true to your intentions for seventy-two hours. After six weeks, the new healthy pattern takes hold.

Step Five: Filling the Void

Habits fulfill needs. To drop an unwanted behavior, you must replace it with one that is nourishing, or you will be left defining yourself as an ex-addict. As you bring influences into your life that support your emotional and physical well-being, sustainable comfort and harmony will take the place of the temporary relief your habit provided.

- Substitute herbal teas and fresh juices for your daily coffee.
- Chew on a natural cinnamon stick instead of putting a cigarette in your mouth.
- Practice a relaxation technique or meditation to shift gears after work instead of your evening cocktail.
- Schedule a regular exercise time each afternoon to release your frustrations rather than yelling at your kids.
- Listen to music while taking a hot bath instead of vegetating in front of the television.

Step Six: Create New Associations

Codependency is a common phrase in psychological circles. It refers to relationships that are so intertwined that every move one person makes deeply affects the other. One person's self-worth is dependent upon the approval of the other. One person's words and actions are in constant reference to the other. One person's relationships, values and interests are so woven into another's that the boundaries between their identities are blurred.

Although there are states of codependency that are clearly unhealthy, in reality we are all codependent. Each of us is constantly exchanging thoughts and feelings with those around us, absorbing and releasing attitudes, beliefs, emotions, perceptions and interpretations. If you surround yourself with people who are workaholics, you are more likely to take on their traits. If you live with people interested in organic nutrition, you are more likely to be influenced by their beliefs and behaviors. If you recognize the need to stop smoking marijuana, but continue to live with roommates who get high every day, it will be more difficult (though not impossible) to stay your course.

Human beings want to belong and demonstrate their connection to a tribe or community by participating in behaviors that characterize the clan. Freeing yourself from a toxic behavior may require that you put some distance between you and members of the group who continue to participate. This is often one of the most difficult obstacles to freeing yourself from enslaving habits and regaining authenticity.

To the extent possible, seek out relationships and communities that reinforce your commitment to life-promoting choices. It can be as simple as choosing to eat in healthier restaurants rather than fast-food franchises, joining a fitness club and participating in Pilates classes, or attending a meditation workshop. Authenticity begins with an intention but manifests with the exercise of new choices.

Authentic Ownership

Children love playing with toys. Take a three-year-old into a toy store, and the child will immediately declare ownership over a doll, a truck or a ball. If another kid tries to take the plaything away, the object's value increases and efforts to assert possession rights escalate. If, however, the process is allowed to unfold without competition or interference, the child will tire of the original toy within a short period of time and become enamored by a new one.

We are born into a material world, and it is our birthright to enjoy abundance. The universe is an expression of abundance. Our challenge is to enjoy the world, without allowing our peace and well-being to be held hostage to the acquisition of things.

Material things can take on the status of graven images if you overinvest your emotional energy in the acquisition of stuff. "I'll be happy once I move into my new house." "I can't wait until I get my new car." "I'll feel good about myself once I can fit into this outfit." You know by now that more stuff will not make you happy.

When it comes to material possessions, neither over-investing nor feigning a lack of interest in the material world contributes to authenticity. Take a survey of your stuff. Do you have enough? Too much? Not enough? What would need to change for you to have enough? If you have the sense that your material possessions own you, rather than you owning them, it is probably a signal to simplify.

Enjoy your stuff and enjoy yourself. Take walks in the woods. Go on bike rides. Spend time playing with your pets or children. Enjoy intimate conversations with friends. Enjoy the world of people and things without making ownership your driving force.

Authentically Complex

If hypocrisy is the discrepancy between what we say and what we do, then we are all hypocrites. We may present ourselves as fervent environmentalists but fail to recycle a plastic bag. We may espouse our commitment to healthy eating, but indulge in French fries and a milkshake. We may champion the principles of nonviolence and then engage in a vigorous argument with someone who disagrees with our point of view.

Authenticity does not demand perfection, for if it did there would be no authentic people living on earth. Human beings embody contradictory values. Authenticity requires that we embrace our incongruities and ambiguities while doing our best to make choices that reflect our core values. Whenever our deeds are misaligned with our beliefs or expressed desires, we have the opportunity to make new choices that bring us back to who we want to be.

When our minds are quiet, we can more clearly hear our inner voice calling us home to a place of unshakable authenticity. From this place, we serve ourselves and those with whom we share our lives.

I demonstrate my commitment to authenticity by:

1) Identifying habits of behavior that do not reflect my core values and consciously replacing them with choices that do.

2) Asking myself how I would like to see the next chapter in my life unfold and taking steps in alignment with that vision.

3) Looking at my material world and aligning it with my values by finding balance between simplicity and abundance.

THE THIRD COMMITMENT:
I COMMIT TO ACCEPTANCE

Thou shalt not take the name
of the Lord thy God in vain.
Exodus 20:7

Everyone
Is God speaking.
Why not be polite and
Listen to Him?
Hafiz

"Damn! The company renting my condo is reporting their payments to the IRS, and now I'll have to pay taxes on the income. My thirty-year-old daughter announces she is divorcing her husband and wants to move back into my home with her two kids. To top things off, yesterday someone sideswiped my car. If there is a God, he doesn't give a damn about me."

Sometimes life goes the way we want it to, and sometimes it does not. When everything is flowing according to our ideas of how things should be, we feel in harmony with our environment and the universe. When there is lack of alignment between what we want and how things are unfolding, we experience disharmony and stress. When our frustration reaches the boiling point, we may lash out with words and actions at the people around us or at God. The proscription to "not take the name of the Lord in vain"—to not curse your circumstance—can be reformulated to "commit to acceptance of the present moment."

Time is a human notion. We observe that babies emerge

from but do not return to the womb and that the broken shards of a shattered glass do not come back together. We cannot go back. Our concept of time reflects the flow of our thoughts. One thought after another gives us the experience of time.

If you become aware of the thoughts that arise and fade in your mind, you will notice that each is a consideration of something that either happened in the past or may occur in the future. You may be aware of a conversation you had yesterday or an event you attended last month. Alternatively, you may be thinking about something you want or fear will happen: a pending graduation, a move to a new town, a court appearance. Your mind, through the generation of thoughts, creates the experience of past and future through memories and anticipations.

Recalling the past, you may remember an experience with joy or remorse. Projecting into the future, you may anticipate an experience with enthusiasm or trepidation. Your interpretations define your experience of life. If you allow past losses or mistakes to dominate your mind, or if you live constantly with the anticipation of something yet to come, you are fettered to something over which you have limited influence. To live in peace, you must release the past, be open to the future and accept the present as it is.

It's easy to practice acceptance when things are going well. It is more challenging when they are not. The commitment to practicing acceptance includes accepting that there will be times when it may be difficult to accept the way things are. Although these times may be difficult, they are opportunities for tremendous personal growth.

Release Resistance

According to modern science, our universe did not exist until 13.7 billion years ago when a point of ignition sparked the Big Bang. The original eruption released particles of matter and antimatter, the vast majority of which completely annihilated each other within the first nanoseconds of creation. About one in a billion particles avoided this obliteration, leading to the formation of elementary building blocks: photons, neutrons, quarks and electrons. Just a few minutes after its birth, the universe cooled enough for these high-intensity particles to begin interacting, first forming hydrogen and then heavier elements.

Over the next 9 billion years, more complex atoms and molecules came into existence, until about 5 billion years ago, when vast clouds of particles began compressing into star systems. Our sun, a fairly average-sized star, is one of approximately 200 billion nuclear reactors in the Milky Way galaxy. Our nearest galactic neighbor is the Andromeda galaxy, which contains about 300 billion stars. Our global neighborhood, which includes about 30 galaxies, comprises the "local group," which is one tiny component of a "local supercluster" that includes about six thousand galaxies. If your mind is spinning, you've been paying attention.

Coming back to earth, it took about a billion years before the first one-celled life-forms appeared in the primordial oceans. Sponges showed up about 600 million years ago, insects arrived 450 million years ago and egg-laying reptiles crawled onto land about 300 million years ago. Mammals came into power about 65 million years ago.

Our distant human relatives stood up on two legs about three million years ago in Africa. Individuals who could pass for modern humans began the technological climb about 200,000 years ago. Your human genes go back about eight thousand generations.

The DNA that intertwined to form you resulted from the merging of one of your mother's 300,000 eggs with one of the nearly half a billion sperm cells that were released by your father during a single act of lovemaking. Before and since the moment of your conception, an incalculable number of events have unfolded throughout your life for you to reach this moment.

When you resist what is happening in this moment, you are resisting the entire flow of life. I encourage you to practice acceptance of this moment, because considering what you are up against (the entire universe from the beginning of time), resistance is unlikely to be successful.

Accept the Now

Several years ago, I had a friend from India who was a *sannyasi*, or monk. We called him Swamaji. He traveled around the world, staying a few days or weeks with people who benefited from his wisdom, compassion and light-hearted nature.

One day I received a collect call from Swamaji, who was in the coronary care unit at Columbia University Medical School in New York City. At the age of forty-two years old, he had developed sudden chest pain, was rushed to the emergency room and within hours underwent coronary artery bypass surgery. I was shocked to hear of his situation since he had none of the usual risk factors for early heart disease. He never smoked, was a lifelong vegetarian, got lots of exercise as he walked everywhere, and he never lost his enthusiastic outlook on life.

He was his usual cheerful self, even as he spoke to me from his hospital bed. I seemed more concerned about his condition than he was. When I asked him why he sounded so happy, he replied in his sweet, lilting Indian accent, "I'm having a most wonderful time. The doctors are very attentive. The nurses are so kind—they even bathe me. I'm served food several times per day, and I get to talk to medical students, who seem very interested in my life."

I was still having trouble understanding why he was not feeling any anxiety, considering the seriousness of his condition. He proceeded to tell me, "I had been staying with a wealthy family on Long Island, whose children wanted to ride the roller coasters at Coney Island. A few weeks ago we drove in the family's Mercedes to the amusement park. I found it particularly amusing that we traveled in a car known for its smooth ride, only to pay for the experience of a very bumpy ride on the Cyclone. I realized that people enjoy roller coasters because despite the jostling and the appearance of danger, riders know they will be safe in the end."

He continued, "This is how I live my life. I am deeply connected to a place of divinity within me that has no beginnings or endings. Regardless of what happens, I know I am safe because the real me is not bound in time and space. The real me is in this world, but not of this world. Therefore, I have committed my life to relaxing and enjoying the ride."

Accepting life as it unfolds does not imply that we relinquish our desires for things to be different. We would not do or accomplish anything if we relinquished our needs, goals and intentions. Spirituality does not imply inaction. Spiritually oriented people are very action oriented. Think of Buddha, Mahatma Gandhi, Martin Luther King Jr. or Mother Teresa. Established in their deep connection to the sacred, they worked relentlessly to improve the world.

Acceptance means focusing on the present while assessing the choices available to you in this moment. If there are many possibilities, make the choice that is likely to bring the most evolutionary results. If there is only one choice, take it.

If there are no obvious choices, relax and accept the fact that for now, you cannot do anything.

Feel the Body

Over thirty years ago, I participated in a meditation training program with Maharishi Mahesh Yogi. During the 1960s he was one of the first teachers from India to become popular in the West and became famous as the "Beatles guru." During extended meditation sessions, participants would often have dramatic emotional experiences. Some people would feel they were reliving an intense traumatic incident from childhood, while others might have extreme mood fluctuations triggered by apparently insignificant circumstances.

Disciples would often describe their experiences to Maharishi in elaborate detail. He would listen patiently to their stories until they finished speaking. Pausing before responding, he gave the impression that he was about to provide deep insight to resolve their confusion and relieve their anguish. But more often than not, Maharishi's counsel was uncomplicated. He would simply say, "Feel the body."

Feeling the body means bringing your attention to the physical sensations it is generating and listening without resistance. It is among the most powerful techniques for bringing your attention into the present moment—into the now. The body resides in the present. The mind lives in the past and the future. When you bring your attention to your body, your judging mind quiets and your still observer becomes more available.

Resistance to pain often intensifies the discomfort. Whether we are receiving an immunization as a child or a root canal as an adult, fear and tension surrounding the procedure magnifies our distress. Assuming that no immediate action will avoid the pain, relaxing into the experience—into the moment—is the most effective way to move through it.

The Uncomfortable Now, the Possible Future

The present moment is not always easy to accept, but learning to listen to the sensations your body is generating and hearing the message they are sending reduces distress and ultimately enables you to benefit from the experience. The following process is helpful in processing uncomfortable feelings.

1) Accept the present.

Tune into your environment and your body. Begin by listening to the sounds around you. Become aware of the cars passing by on the street, the hum of the air conditioner in the background and the sound of your own breath. Become aware of the sensations in your body—the feeling of the chair on your bottom, the shoes on your feet, the collar around your neck. Bring your attention to the passage of air through your nostrils, noticing the subtle aromas of your environment and your own body. Continue observing the inflow and outflow of your breath, allowing it to bring you into this moment.

2) Accept your body's signals.

Become aware of the internal sensations in your body—emptiness in your gut, aching in your heart, constriction in your throat. Although these may not be comfortable sensations, feel them without resistance. If sadness wells up, allow yourself to feel it. If anger wells up, allow it to move through your body and release it with your exhalations.

3) Accept responsibility.

Although there are clearly times in life when things happen over which we have no apparent control, most of our daily struggles are the consequences of choices we have made. Acceptance of our personal contribution to the challenges we face helps us recognize that we can make new choices that lead to new possibilities. Can you accept some responsibility for the situation in which you find yourself?

4) Accept change.

Human beings have free will, although we do not often exercise it. Times of challenge are difficult but important opportunities to change habits that may have outlived their value. The question is "What can I *now* do differently?"

5) Commit.

Analyzing the patterns that create distress has value up to a point. People can spend years in therapy learning why they continue making unhealthy choices. Analyzing, explaining and rationalizing can become habits unto themselves. The change we want comes from the new *choices* we are prepared to make.

Seeds of Transformation

Think about a time in your past when you experienced a loss. It may have been the loss of a relationship, a job or money in an investment that caused you emotional pain. Consider your life now and you will probably be aware that the loss, which at the time seemed devastating, allowed for new opportunities to emerge. Had the loss not occurred, the love or abundance you subsequently experienced would not have been possible.

Lauren's job as a senior manager in an investment company was abruptly eliminated as the organization unexpectedly downsized. She felt anger, anxiety, insecurity and depression for the next several months. When no similar position materialized, she decided to take a role with a smaller company, which required that she develop her own client base.

Two years later, she is happier than she ever was working in a large organization. She appreciates the greater control she has over her own life and the more fulfilling relationships she has developed with staff and clients. She is making almost as much money as before with less pressure to sell products that she does not believe are in the best interest of her clients.

You may have been in an intense relationship that you believed would lead to marriage when you discovered your partner was unfaithful. Overwhelmed with grief, rage and disappointment, you wondered how you would survive this loss. A year later you meet a person with whom you resonate physically, emotionally, intellectually and spiritually, and three years later you are happily married to your best friend. Incidentally, you learn that your two-timing ex has already been married and divorced.

It is often easier to recognize retrospectively how accepting rather than resisting what arrives is the best attitude. Developing the inner attitude of "Thy will be done" is worth the practice.

There will of course be times when it does not appear that any good can come from loss or pain. The death of a child or loved one, a devastating accident and natural disasters are a few examples of situations when we are challenged to our core to understand their redeeming purpose. There are no simple or pat answers to these heartbreaking and life-altering events. Still, we must create meaning in order to go on living. Each day, I see people who transform adversity into purpose: parents who lose children to a genetic disease start support groups for others going through similar anguish; survivors of natural disasters commit to helping others rebuild their lives. The next step in life will never return us to our prior state, but I encourage you to look for and nurture the seeds of rebirth in the ashes of loss. There is no other viable life-affirming alternative.

Intend the Change

During heavy storms a river overflowed its banks, prompting local authorities to call for voluntary evacuation of a nearby rural town. Two men in a pickup truck drove by a house on the outskirts of town where Sam Smith was sitting on his porch.

"Sam. Get going! You're going to be flooded out."

"I'm staying right here," Sam replied. "I have my faith in the Lord and he won't let me down."

"Suit yourself," the men said. "You're taking a big risk."

The waters continued rising. Two men in a motorboat cruised by Sam, who was now sitting on his roof.

"Sam. What are you doing? The banks are overflowing and you're asking for trouble."

"I'm not moving," Sam answered. "I have my faith in the Lord and he won't let me down."

The men sped away, shaking their heads.

The waters continued to rise. Two men in a helicopter flew to Sam's place. He was now standing on the top of his chimney, with water up to his knees.

"Sam. This is your last chance. There is no other way you can survive this flood. Get into the helicopter!" the men pleaded.

"I am not going anywhere," Sam asserted. "I have my faith in the Lord and he won't let me down."

A few minutes later, Sam was washed off his roof and drowned in the turbulent waters. Since he was basically an honest man, he found himself at the gates of heaven, filled with righteous indignation and demanding an audience with God.

"I can't believe you let me drown!" Sam bellowed. "I put my faith in you and you let me down."

God replied, "Sam, I didn't let you down. First I sent you two guys in a truck, then I sent two guys in a boat, and finally I sent two guys in a helicopter. I can't help it that you're so stubborn you're only willing to accept my help your way."

When your present moment is generating signals of discomfort, listen to the information and use it to make positive changes. Accepting the present does not imply wallowing in situations or circumstances you can improve. Freedom to respond creatively is a divine gift. Use it.

Metabolize the Past

We are the sum total of the choices we've made. Despite our best intentions, we've made choices that, in retrospect, appear to have been wrong. We may have become involved in relationships or business ventures that created unanticipated pain. Carrying hurt, frustration, hostility, resentment or regret drags us into the past, hampering our ability to enjoy the present. If you had a furious and hurtful argument with your sibling the last time your family came together, you will approach the prospect of another encounter with anxiety or loathing. The incompletely metabolized past pollutes the present. Take time at the end of every day to practice this recapitulation ritual so you do not carry unnecessary pain from today into tomorrow.

Before going to sleep, sit up in your bed, close your eyes and simply observe the inflow and outflow of your breath for five minutes to quiet your mind. Then perform an internal body scan. Sequentially bring your attention to your belly, stomach, heart and throat. Notice any sensations that may be lingering at the end of your day. Use these feelings to bring experiences into your awareness that you have incompletely processed.

Having identified an experience that is still generating residual feelings, determine what more would be necessary to put the issue to rest. This most often requires a commitment on your part to say or do something in order to complete the process. As an example, while performing your body scan, you become aware of a tense feeling in your gut. You realize that you are still feeling irritated over an exchange between you and one of your coworkers, in which she said something critical about someone else on your team. Asking yourself the question "What must I do to resolve this issue?" you recognize that you are feeling uncomfortable because you did not respond in defense of the criticized person at the time. Commit to talking with your coworker first thing in the morning to express your honest perspective.

Sometimes the action required may involve your taking responsibility or offering an apology. In other situations, it may simply require you to express your true feelings. The answer to the question "What must I do to resolve this issue?" will come to you if you take time to quiet your mental turbulence and ask your inner mind for guidance.

Accept Yourself

This planet is a school for evolution of the soul. If we already knew everything, there would be no reason to attend classes here. Do not add insult to injury by beating yourself up over choices that seemed right at the time, but appear incredibly ill conceived in retrospect. Apparent errors in judgment often provide the most valuable lessons, expanding your capacity for humility and compassion. Remember, everyone is doing their best at every moment based upon their current state of consciousness. This means that you are doing your best, even if the consequences of your choices did not meet with your expectations. Be accepting of yourself, reinforcing your acceptance with the commitment to learn from your experiences. Then honor your commitment by making new choices that demonstrate the wisdom you have gained from your expensive lessons.

I demonstrate my commitment to acceptance by:

1) Listening to my body and noticing where I am resisting.

2) Being fully present with the choices available to me.

3) Reminding myself on a regular basis that everyone is doing their best from their level of awareness.

THE FOURTH COMMITMENT:

I COMMIT TO RELAX

Remember the Sabbath day to keep it holy.
Exodus 20:8

Just sit there right now.
Don't do a thing.
Just rest.
For your separation from God
Is the hardest work in this world.
Hafiz

Take a deep breath. Relax. Enter into the present moment. Your breathing, so fundamental to life, is a perpetual reminder of nature's commitment to relax and act. You inhale then pause; you exhale then pause, marking the course of your life from the first inhalation at the time of your birth to the last exhalation at the time of your death.

Your heart contracts and relaxes beginning twenty-two days after conception and continuing until the end of your life. Your digestive tract, from stomach to colon, is continuously contracting and relaxing while moving food along the path from intake to elimination. Wherever you look within your body, the rhythms of nature are expressed in the ebb and flow of life.

The universe operates in cycles and rhythms. The earth whirls on its axis at a thousand miles per hour while circling the sun sixty times faster. The moon dances around the earth every twenty-eight days while performing its own rotational pirouette in the same time period. Our sun, along with its passenger planets (including the earth), revolves around the center of the Milky Way galaxy every 220 million years, which means that human beings have been riding the planet for only 1/1000th of a galactic spin.

Life expresses an innate rhythmicity. Rest and activity are essential building blocks of evolution. Honoring the rhythm of life is key to health and happiness.

The Biology of Time

From one-celled amoebas to trillion-celled humans, the dance of life includes the alternation of pause and play. The scientific study of these rhythmic patterns is called chronobiology. "Chrono" comes from the Greek word *khronos* meaning time, while *bio* is Greek for life. Chronobiology, then, is the study of time in living beings. The core discovery of this emerging scientific field is that living things have internal clocks. These natural timekeepers continuously pulse to innate rhythms, developed over millions of years of evolutionary time.

Back in the 1700s a French astronomer, Jean Jacques de Mairan, observed that mimosa plants opened and closed their leaves at predictable times during the day. Although he assumed the plants were responding to sunlight, he kept some specimens in total darkness and to his surprise, found that they continued opening and closing their leaves as if on an internal timer.

The animal kingdom similarly marches to hidden drummers.

The internal clocks of migratory birds and monarch butterflies send their signals to begin moving with remarkable consistency. The visits of honeybees to pollen-rich flower fields are more precisely timed than your postman's delivery route. Groundhogs emerge from hibernation in early February, halfway between the winter solstice and the spring equinox. From the reproductive cycles of insects to the sleep/wake patterns of rodents, intrinsic biological clocks keep time.

Daily Rhythms

The primary clock of your body measures out a twenty-four-hour day. The pulse of hormones, the rise and fall of stomach acid production, peaks and troughs in body temperature and fluctuations in blood pressure all follow a cycle that is tuned into the rising and setting of the sun. The technical term for these rhythms is *"circadian,"* derived from the Latin words *circa*, meaning around, and *diem*, meaning day.

Every physiological function has a peak time of expression. Between midnight and six in the morning, you have surges of growth hormone, melatonin and prolactin, hormones important in rejuvenation, repair and immune health. Between six o'clock in the morning and noon, your blood pressure and heart rate rise in association with pulses of the hormones adrenaline, renin and angiotensin. Between noon and six in the evening your red blood cell count hits its peak, along with your insulin level and breathing capacity.

Cholesterol levels and urinary flow reach their highest levels between six and ten in the evening, while your stomach acid secretion peaks close to midnight.

Although these patterns developed within the context of the sun rising and setting, your body has internalized the timing so that even if you are completely removed from the normal cues of day and night, your circadian rhythms march on. Research suggests that pacemaker cells in the hypothalamus of the brain coordinate both your hormonal system and involuntary nervous system. They are closely linked to your pineal gland, which makes and secretes the hormone melatonin, important in the regulation of sleep and wakefulness.

The majority of health challenges also follow a circadian pattern. The pain of arthritis and the melancholy of depression are most pronounced around six in the morning. Heart attacks strike most often at 9 A.M. as people are starting their workdays. Tension headaches tend to come on at four in the afternoon, whereas migraine headaches start most commonly at four in the morning. Gout attacks choose midnight to assault, while stomach ulcer and gallbladder pain wait until two in the morning. Even the illnesses that bring misery cannot escape from the rhythms of nature.

Vitality and enthusiasm are the fruits of a life in harmony with the rhythms of nature. Engage in dynamic action and take time to relax. These are keys to successful living.

Optimal Daily Routine

Simple lamps burning olive, castor bean or fish oil can be found in Egyptian archaeological sites, demonstrating that people have attempted to extend their active hours beyond sunset for thousands of years. The early part of the nineteenth century saw the first widespread use of gas lamps, which required lamplighters to light and extinguish the lanterns each evening and morning. It wasn't until the late 1800s that Thomas Edison demonstrated the practical value of an incandescent lightbulb, allowing people to stay awake all night if they chose.

Some researchers have suggested that people can be assigned to a *chronotype*, for example "morning larks" or "night owls." In a study of college students classified as morning or evening types, those who went to bed and arose earlier had more consistent sleep, required fewer naps during the day and reported fewer physical health complaints than those who stayed up late and slept in the next day.

From an Ayurvedic perspective, Benjamin Franklin's prescription for health, wealth and wisdom—retire and arise early—was right on target. Align your daily routine with the rhythms of your environment to regain and maintain mental clarity, emotional stability and physical vitality.

Morning

6:00 A.M. Awake at sunrise. Leave your shades or curtains partially open. Avoid, if possible, starting your day with the shock of an alarm clock.

6:05 A.M. Empty your bladder. Drink a cup of warm water to stimulate your bowels.

6:10 A.M. Perform your morning hygiene routine— shower, brush your teeth, clean your tongue.

6:30 A.M. Perform a few minutes of stretching.

6:45 A.M. Meditate or relax for ten to twenty minutes.

7:15 A.M. Exercise for thirty minutes.

7:45 A.M. Eat breakfast, if you are hungry.

Afternoon and Evening

Noon Eat lunch, followed by a walk.

5:00 P.M. Meditate or relax for ten to twenty minutes.

6:00 P.M. Eat dinner, followed by a walk.

7:00 P.M. Keep evening activities light and enjoyable.

10:00 P.M. Get into bed with the lights out.

Meditate—Quiet Your Mind, Rest Your Body

Silence is a rare commodity in modern life. Wherever you are right now, close your eyes and listen to the sounds around you. If you listen for a few minutes, the chances are you will hear a considerable amount of background noise;

people speaking, traffic moving, dogs barking, appliances humming. The modern world is filled with sounds.

Even if you are in a quiet place, you will notice there are sounds disturbing the silence. These are the sounds of your mind, with its constant inner conversation. The mind is a thought-generating organ, which can disturb your peace, whether or not your neighbors are having a party.

Quieting your mind provides the opportunity to change direction. Otherwise, you are likely to think and act according to established patterns. For example, you see an advertisement for a business where you used to work. This triggers memories of your old boss. You remember how frustrated you felt working for him. This evokes uncomfortable churning sensations in your gut. This cascade of thoughts and feelings in your mind and body takes on a life of its own and disturbs your peace. Learning to quiet this inner thought traffic enables you to break the cycle.

Meditation is technology to access the silence. Before and after every thought-wave of the mind, the ocean of awareness is silent. Most of the time, thoughts are coming so fast and furiously, you do not notice the deep stillness that gives rise to the activity of the mind. As a result of mental turbulence, your mind becomes anxious and your body becomes agitated.

There are many different meditation techniques, each of which can open a door into a quiet mind. Chanting, listening to music, free-form dancing, observing ocean waves break against the shore or listening to a flowing river can temporarily still the chatter of an active mind, providing a glimpse of the silent space between the thoughts.

If you have not previously learned to meditate, try this simple technique that uses the breath and a breathing mantra. Having taught meditation for over thirty years, I have learned that people are more likely to practice meditation and gain its benefits if instructed by a qualified teacher. We do not expect children to learn how to swim, ride a bike or play the piano from a book. There are some things in life that are still best taught face-to-face with a teacher, and meditation is one of them. A list of qualified Chopra Center meditation teachers can be accessed through our Web site (see page 197). In the meantime, here is a simple starter meditation.

- Sit comfortably, close your eyes, and begin observing the inflow and outflow of your breath.
- As you are inhaling, silently say the sound "So."
- As you are exhaling, silently say the sound "Hum."
- When you find that your attention has drifted away from So Hum, gently return your attention to the mantra.
- Continue like this for about ten minutes (you can peek at a clock when you think the time has passed), and then take another couple of minutes before opening your eyes.

There are only a few possible experiences you can have while meditating. Your awareness can be with the mantra, your awareness can be engaged in a stream of thoughts, or your awareness can slip between the thoughts, allowing you glimpses of a silent mind. If your body is tired and you have not been sleeping soundly, you can also fall asleep while meditating.

The basic principle for effective meditation is that whenever you realize you are not thinking the mantra, gently bring your awareness back to it. Relaxation is relinquishing the need to control. Meditation is a direct way to practice this skill.

Sleep—The Nursemaid to Humanity

At least twenty-five million Americans didn't sleep well last night. Almost half of people over the age of sixty-five have chronic sleeping problems. You may have trouble falling asleep, trouble staying asleep or simply sense you are not sleeping soundly. Poor nighttime sleep is associated with increased anxiety, depression, accidents and missed work. You need deep rest to perform at your best.

Insomnia results from your mind refusing to let go. Ruminating over something from the past or worrying about or planning something in the future engages the mind, even though the body is tired and craves rest. Restful sleep is an expression of a life in harmony with nature. Getting up early, meditating twice daily, eating healthy meals at appropriate times and engaging in regular exercise are important contributors to restful nighttime sleep. If despite an otherwise healthy lifestyle, you are still not sleeping soundly, try making a few changes as you prepare for bed.

- Eat a lighter dinner and take a walk afterward.
- While preparing for bed, run a warm bath, adding a few drops of lavender aroma oil to the bathwater.
- Perform a slow, gentle oil massage to your head and feet.
- Soak in the tub for fifteen minutes while listening to soothing music.
- Drink four to six ounces of warm milk with a quarter teaspoon of nutmeg, or drink a cup of calming herbal tea, such as chamomile, valerian, hops or skullcap.
- Write in a journal about anything that is activating your mind.
- Read relaxing material for a few minutes.
- Turn off the lights, close your eyes and observe your breathing until you fall asleep.

Massage Yourself to Sleep

Briefly massaging your head and feet can prepare you for restful sleep. Using a tablespoon of warm oil, soothingly massage your forehead from side to side with your palm. Gently massage your temples, then the outside of your ears. Spend a little time massaging the back and front of your neck.

With a second tablespoon of oil, slowly but firmly massage the soles of your feet. Work the oil around your toes with your fingertips. Sit quietly for a few moments to soak in the oil, then remove the excess oil with a warm washcloth.

Solar Rhythms

The journey of the earth around the sun influences your mind and body. Because the earth is tilted on its axis, the number of sunlight hours varies dramatically from season to season. On June 21, the summer solstice, a day in Los Angeles is nearly five hours longer than on the shortest winter day, December 21. The change in daylight hours as the earth makes its annual pilgrimage around the sun results in seasons that affect every living being on earth.

People are influenced by this waxing and waning light exposure. Many studies since the 1980s have confirmed the phenomena of Seasonal Affective Disorder (SAD). As the days get shorter, a significant number of people report symptoms of fatigue and depression, which improve once daylight hours increase. People with SAD often report weight gain during the winter months, associated with strong carbohydrate cravings. SAD patients may be instructed to sit in front of bright lights for several hours a day, which results in some improvement in their symptoms.

You may notice subtle shifts in your moods with changes in the seasons. You may tend to be more inwardly oriented as the leaves drop in autumn, more reclusive during winter months, more amorous during the lush spring and more outgoing during summer days. Your mind and body reflect the natural cycles of life.

Acknowledge and honor the different faces of nature as she rotates through her seasonal changes. If possible, rather than fighting her introverted and extroverted moods see if you can align yourself with them. During the shorter winter days, try the following:

- Go to bed earlier, and allow yourself to get more rest, if needed.
- Sleep in later on the weekends.
- Take time to meditate in the early morning and later afternoon.
- Eat warmer, heavier foods like soups and stews.
- Drink hot gingerroot tea throughout the day (one teaspoon of fresh ginger per cup of hot water).
- Use pungent spices liberally.
- Exercise earlier in the day.
- Take hot baths and saunas.
- Find some great reading material to read in the evening rather than watching television.

During longer summer days, the extra hours of sunlight predispose to overheating, overexposure and overactivity. Balance these tendencies by:

- Drinking plenty of fluids, such as water and juices.
- Eating lighter.
- Consuming abundant quantities of fresh fruits and vegetables.
- Wearing lighter clothing; wearing sunblock.
- Avoiding being outdoors during the hottest midday hours.
- Being around and getting into water.

Lunar Rhythms

The moon has been the object of attention for lovers, poets and sky gazers since human beings first looked to the heavens. In many ancient cultures, the moon represents the feminine aspect of nature, balancing the masculine sun. The word menstruation is derived from the Greek word *mene*, meaning moon. Since a woman's menstrual cycle and the lunar cycle both average twenty-eight days, the moon has traditionally been associated with fertility and emotions.

Scientific studies have suggested that there may be some creditability to this claim, with more women having their periods during the new moon phase than at other times of the lunar cycle. Peak fertility has been associated with the third quarter of the moon phase, raising the possibility that the waning light after a full moon may precipitate ovulation.

Most women are aware of fluctuations in their minds and bodies during a monthly cycle, and scientific research has confirmed that women tend to be more emotionally and sexually receptive around ovulation than in the week prior to menstruation. Irritability, anxiety, depression, tiredness and conflicted interactions are not uncommon in the premenstrual time period, with a small percentage of women feeling distressed enough to require medical intervention.

Traditionally, the period immediately prior to and during menstruation is an inward time for women. According to Ayurveda, menstruation is an important detoxifying process, which enables women to purify and rejuvenate on a monthly basis.

Honor this natural feminine cycle. Schedule a lighter schedule on the day you are anticipating your period. Drink plenty of
fluids. Prepare fresh, nourishing meals. Reduce the intensity of
your exercise routine, favoring yoga or walks rather than a vigorous workout. If you can, get a massage. Avoid engaging in argu-
ments. Try to be in bed by ten o'clock. In modern society, you
may not have the luxury of staying home from your job for a
couple days, but at the least, avoid unnecessarily overworking.

Calm, Focused Attention

Your desires, intentions and needs engage your body,
mind and soul. In your effort to acquire, achieve or attain,
you become consumed with the goal—be it a relationship, a
business deal or a material possession. Maintaining focused
attention is a crucial component in fulfilling your desires,
but it is only half the story. Letting go is the other essential
ingredient for successful living. Temporarily releasing your
attachment to the fruits of your desires enhances the likelihood that you will achieve that which you seek.

When you allow yourself to relax, your awareness expands.
In this expansion, you see things in a broader way that was
not possible when you were caught up in the desire.
Alternating intense, engaged focus with expanded, relaxed
awareness enables you to fine-tune the trajectory to achieve
your goals. Honor the natural rhythms of action and relaxation. This is a timeless formula for success and happiness.

I demonstrate my commitment to relax by:

1) Taking time to quiet my mind on a daily basis in meditation.

2) Taking steps to ensure restful sleep at night.

3) Paying attention to the seasons, cycles and rhythms of my natural environment.

THE FIFTH
COMMITMENT:
I COMMIT TO WHOLENESS

Honor thy father and thy mother, in order that thy
days may be prolonged upon the land which the
Lord thy God giveth thee.

Exodus 20:12

The admission price to hear
The lofty minstrels speak of love
Is affordable only to those
Who have not exhausted themselves
Dividing God all day
And thus need rest.

Hafiz

Spirituality calls us to reconcile opposite values, and there is no more fundamental duality than masculine and feminine. Our society is engaged in an unprecedented conversation about sex. Previously unchallenged ideas about families and the roles played by men and women are being tested in new experiments. Single-parent families, same-sex marriages, merged stepfamilies, unmarried coparenting, divorced coparenting—these phenomena were not ones that engaged our grandparents' attention.

Only recently have these fundamental issues emerged into a dialogue about what it means to be a woman and a man. Society responds vigorously when a long-standing conviction is challenged, and new ideas about sexuality are eliciting strong responses. A spiritual approach requires us to bring peace to the conflict by finding unity in the diversity.

The fifth commitment honors the essence of mother and father by embracing wholeness—the feminine and masculine power that resides within us. In the Tantric tradition of India, the universe is seen as the continuous dance between male and female energies. Feminine Shakti is the maternal power of the universe, giving birth to form and phenomena. Masculine Shiva is pure, detached and self-absorbed. Passionate Shakti merging with remote Shiva engenders the cosmos and all sentient beings.

Our understanding of men and women in Western culture is a complicated affair. The story of our primordial father and mother, Adam and Eve, raises more questions than it answers. God made man in his image on the sixth day of creation and placed him in the Garden of Eden. The first human, separated from God, was incomplete, so from Adam's side God made woman.

For reasons that only God understands, Adam is told not to eat the fruit from the Tree of Knowledge of Good and Evil. Then the original intersex miscommunication apparently occurred, for Eve told the serpent that God said they should neither eat of nor *touch* the tree. When the snake convinced her to take the fruit and then shared it with Adam.

With their eyes of self-awareness opened, they became conscious of their nakedness, leading to the first fashion statement. One can almost hear Eve asking, "Does this leaf look good on me?" God confronted Adam, Adam blamed Eve, Eve blamed the snake, and all parties to the crime were punished. God evicted Adam and Eve from the Garden before they had a chance to eat from the Tree of Life, which would have made them immortal.

Almost immediately after leaving the Garden, our primal

parents had two sons, who promptly demonstrated the meaning of sibling rivalry. After slaying his brother, Cain somehow finds a wife, has a son and a few thousand generations later, we are here to contemplate what this myth about man and woman means to us. The story we tell about the original man and woman is complex. Relationships between men and women remain complex to this day.

The Sexual Spectrum

Girls are different from boys. During the late sixties many believed that nurture was more influential than nature. This belief led to parents making conscious choices to minimize gender-reinforcing stereotypes by encouraging their sons to be more sensitive and their daughters to be more assertive. Still, many parents found that their sons turned every stick into a gun, while their daughters tucked their stuffed animals into cribs at night.

Western society is slowly recognizing that there is a spectrum of masculinity and femininity within which we all fall. It is becoming acceptable for even the most macho athlete, soldier or leading actor to acknowledge his emotional side, while we are seeing steady progress in societal acceptance of women's strong leadership roles in business, politics, entertainment and sports. Embracing the power inherent in our masculine and feminine sides enables us to be whole and powerful.

Exploring the Masculine/ Embracing the Feminine

Your masculine and feminine aspects can manifest in different ways. They can be expressed in a childlike manner, reflecting innocence, enthusiasm and vulnerability. They can show up as adult power, radiating determination, authority and control. They can manifest as wise old sages, embodying the totality of life experience and understanding. Getting to know the rich and diverse masculine and feminine expressions that reside within you deepens your understanding, awakens your intrinsic power and expands your compassion.

Healthy archetypal masculine energy is expressed as confidence, determination, discipline and responsibility. It is resolute and goal oriented. Access to its power provides the foundation for strong, ethical leadership. Unhealthy male energy manifests as stubbornness, oppression, inflexibility and exploitation.

Healthy primordial feminine energy is creative and cyclical. The Greek word for uterus is *metra*, which is related to time and measurement. Creation incubates in and emerges from the womb of the archetypal woman. The feminine force aligns you with the seasons, cycles and rhythms of nature. It can be gently nurturing or fiercely protective, supportive or destructive, encouraging or castrating.

Male or female, we each have masculine and feminine energy in our body, mind and soul. Men and women have different relationships to their masculine and feminine sides, but both benefit by knowing the powerful forces that live within. Women who develop their ability to set and achieve goals experience enhanced self-esteem and are less likely to tolerate demeaning or abusive relationships. Men who develop their nurturing side can take better advantage of their emotional intelligence, which enhances both personal and professional decision making. Awakening these intrinsic potentials enhances our ability to find creative solutions to our individual and collective problems.

Indulge Your Child

Children are open to surprises. A rainbow, caterpillar or balloon provokes waves of joy. The unexpected and the unplanned offer continuous opportunities for a child to feel alive. The innocent mind of the child has not yet developed to the extent that it continuously rehashes the past or anticipates the future. Perpetually in present-moment awareness, a child experiences life as magical and mysterious.

Observe a three-year-old playing in the park. One moment the child is climbing courageously up a jungle gym, testing his limits and raising safety concerns. The next moment he trips over a rock, scrapes his knee and cries for his mother. It is the nature of children to push their boundaries and then want to be comforted instantly whenever they fall short or meet resistance.

Sweet, playful and spontaneous, the internalized child keeps our hearts open. Loving, affectionate and inherently trusting, the archetypal child reminds us of our original innocence. Porous boundaries and total authenticity characterize this delicate aspect of our being, which most of us have learned to protect with sobriety and responsibility.

If throughout childhood your innocence and purity were safeguarded, you learned to set appropriate boundaries while maintaining your sense of self. Optimism about the world and trust in the inherent goodness of people become core beliefs. If, however, your earliest experiences were chaotic and turbulent, it could take a good part of a lifetime to regain wholeness.

When Alex was six years old his father left his mother. Beleaguered with the responsibilities of raising three children, she placed Alex in a Catholic boarding school, confessing, "You're just too much for me to handle now." Although overwhelmed with a sense of loss and loneliness, Alex quickly had to develop a tough skin to avoid further emotional pain from the bullying of his classmates.

From this young age and throughout his adult life, Alex's sole focus in life was not to be dependent on anyone. He became a commercial airline pilot, and although he achieved financial success, his family life was in perpetual turmoil. A year after his third divorce, he developed prostate cancer, which ended his flying career. Although his treatments were successful, and his disability insurance and pension provided him economic security, he found himself in a deep depression that failed to respond adequately to medications.

As he shared with me his painful life story, it became obvious that Alex had never had a real opportunity to be a kid. Needing to maintain constant vigilance just to survive, he was unprepared to enjoy himself, even when his core needs were met. Fortunately, one of his daughters had two young children who loved their grandfather. I encouraged him to spend as much time as possible with them. He began taking his grandkids on frequent outings to amusement parks, baseball games and local beaches. He purchased his first bicycle and started riding regularly with them. Indulging in his grandchildren, Alex found increasing joy in himself.

If you are in tune with your archetypal child, you will spontaneously relate to the world with enthusiasm and playfulness. You anticipate that people will respond positively to your involvement in their lives and are comfortable taking risks. Confident of nurturing love when you need it, you expand your comfort zone, widening your circle of command. You believe you are worthy of attention and project this to everyone you encounter.

Commit to allow your archetypal child to play. Even if your childhood history was one of neglect or trauma, you can heal the innocent being that resides within you. Every soul is worthy of unconditional love and acceptance. Now is the time to begin.

Ask yourself what makes you happy. How can you be more playful? What do you want to do even if it has no practical purpose other than to make you smile or awaken your enthusiasm? Make a list of things that you like to do and carve out time on a regular basis to do them. Here are some suggestions:

- Take a dance class.
- Try watercolor painting.
- Go to an amusement park.
- Walk along the beach and pick up shells.
- Learn to play a musical instrument.
- Play a game of volleyball.
- Eat a hot fudge sundae.
- Go to a toy store.

Notice the signs that alert you when you are insufficiently indulging the childlike aspect of your being:

- You frequently feel offended.
- You withdraw emotionally over minor slights.
- You react aggressively when challenged.
- You are cynical.
- You are inflexible.
- You are distrustful in relationships.
- You seldom laugh.
- You always have something important to do.

Make a commitment to honor the innocence and sweetness that resides in your heart, regardless of your chronological age.

Look for opportunities to express it to your family and friends and to yourself. Treat the people with whom you are most intimate as you would treat an innocent child. Anticipate nothing less in return from the closest people in your life.

Your Inner Adult

The adult human is a heroic being, setting his or her sights on a goal and willing to do what it takes to achieve the objective. Embracing your inner hero enables you to overcome obstacles to fulfill your deepest intentions and desires.

The awakened masculine aspect of a healthy adult adds patience to enthusiasm. Healthy masculine energy maintains focus without rigidity, comfortably establishing and achieving goals while viewing unanticipated obstacles as learning experiences.

Adults with underdeveloped masculine energy blame their shortcomings on others, fate or bad luck. Lacking confidence or determination, they rationalize their failures with tired catchphrases such as, "Nothing really matters in the end," or "I just haven't had the lucky breaks other people get." Alternatively, in an effort to overcompensate for an unhealthy inner masculine force, people become driven in ways that are detrimental to themselves and those around them. Working excessively long hours and always in a hurry, they miss the small but meaningful experiences that connect them intimately with the people in their lives. In their pursuit to overcome their sense of inadequacy, they neglect opportunities to receive love and appreciation from people who love them independently of their accomplishments.

The feminine side of a healthy adult is competent and nurturing, capable of caring for herself and others. Creative and centered, she knows when to be flexible and when to set boundaries. When directed toward the family, the balanced feminine force provides unconditional love and encouragement for all members to reach their full potential. Directed professionally, balanced adult feminine energy manages people effectively without demeaning them and takes satisfaction in the success of others.

Unbalanced feminine energy can result in emotional and physical exhaustion. Driven to care for others to the point of depriving themselves, people with an imbalanced impulse to nurture eventually become depleted. A person with the mind-set "I'm too busy driving to go the gas station" will inevitably run out of gas.

Jungian psychology sees these basic forces as the expression of archetypal energies in the collective mind. A man or woman may assume the guise of the king or queen, who takes charge of situations and acts decisively. The primal force can appear as the untamed god or goddess who stays close to nature by working in the garden, riding horses or hiking in the woods. The primordial inner Adonis or Venus is expressed through sensuality, sexuality and passion. The archetypal face of the healer and nurturer cares for the wounded, children and those in need through selfless giving. The mystic archetype appears as the inward directed force that embraces the psychological and spiritual realms of life.

Get to know the various faces of your inner archetypes. Notice that every expression has both light and dark sides. Recognizing and owning up to both the sacred and the profane aspects of your inner forces enables you to choose more consciously who you want to be in the world.

ARCHETYPAL FACE	QUALITIES
King/Queen	Commanding, competent, forceful Controlling, ruthless, manipulative
Nature Man/Woman	Independent, natural, powerful Indifferent, aloof, primitive
Adonis/Venus	Sensual, romantic, passionate Superficial, materialistic, self-absorbed
Healer/Earth Mother	Nurturing, caring, loving Self-deprecating, indulgent, overbearing
Mystic	Insightful, intuitive, mysterious Detached, unavailable, fatalistic

See if you can acknowledge and embrace the archetypal forces that you have subconsciously rejected. When you feel uncomfortable around people who have interests in areas other than yours, see your discomfort as a signal to find something in that realm you can relate to or support. You may not currently have an interest in business, but see if you can appreciate the focused attention of someone who does. You may not feel attracted to conversations about children, but see if there is something in the discussions that informs you. As you expand your sense of self beyond narrow definitions, you will feel increasingly centered and comfortable in diverse situations and circumstances.

Your Inner Sage

There is a moment in every epic tale when the hero loses his way or encounters an obstacle that seems insurmountable. This is usually the cue for a wise sage to appear, providing guidance and inspiration. The wizard Merlin to young Arthur, Obi-Wan Kenobi to Luke Skywalker, Mr. Miyagi to the Karate Kid, and Gandalf to Frodo are modern examples of the archetypal sage who lives within us all.

The feminine side of the sage is the Wise Old Woman. She appears as the compassionate grandmotherly being who is willing to use her special knowledge and power to make things right. She is the Fairy Godmother to Cinderella and the Good Witch of the North to Dorothy. In normal life she may show up as the grandmother who always makes you feel better or the teacher who says just the right thing to motivate and inspire you. Your inner godmother carries the perfect blend of wisdom and compassion. Even when you've made an obvious error in judgment, she is there to provide comfort and encouragement.

Become intimate with your inner sage. He or she knows what you need and desires only to see you fulfill your destiny in life. To access your inner wisdom, you need to quiet your internal turbulent voices and listen to the truth that comes from your archetypal sage.

Close your eyes, take several slow deep breaths, and envision yourself in a beautiful, sacred place. The air is pure, the sun is shining and a sense of purity, safety and peace pervades the environment. Now imagine your serene, wise being sitting before you beneath a majestic tree. Looking into his or her eyes, you feel unconditional love and compassion. Sit with your inner sage and ask for wisdom and an expanded perspective on any issue you are facing in your life. Through your inner sage, you can access the guidance you are seeking.

I have guided hundreds of people through this simple visualization and have found that almost everyone can envision a wise inner being who provides them with true and beneficial insights about their lives.

Create a relationship with your inner counselor, master, guru, rabbi, teacher or guide. Make the commitment to access and cultivate this fountainhead of inner wisdom. Allow the unconditional acceptance that flows from your sage to permeate your heart and soul. Through this relationship, you will make choices consistent with your highest values. Access to this archetypal energy enables you to tap into the wisdom of your heart.

Honor Your Father and Your Mother

You have many dimensions to your nature. Embracing the totality of what it means to be human enriches every aspect of life. Acknowledging the different expressions of your masculine and feminine power unleashes energy and creativity. The wider you are able to envision yourself, the more accepting you will be of others. Rigid views of gender, sexuality and permissible roles for boys and girls breed judgment and intolerance. We serve the honor of our parents best by radiating kindness, compassion, love and wisdom. Make the commitment to know and love your inner innocent child, powerful adult and wise sage; they comprise the amazingly complex being you are. Commit to wholeness. It is your birthright.

I demonstrate my commitment to wholeness by:

1) Indulging my inner child on a regular basis.

2) Balancing my goals for future success with choices that bring me happiness now.

3) Accessing the wisdom of the ages through my archetypal inner sage.

The Sixth Commitment:

I COMMIT TO FORGIVENESS

Thou shalt not kill.
Exodus 20:13

Forgiveness
Is the cash you need.
All the other kinds of silver really buy
Just strange things.
Hafiz

The Katha Upanishad tells the story of a young boy, Nachiketa. While his father is being honored for donating a herd of cattle to the local temple, Nachiketa calls attention to the fact that the gift is not as generous as it seems as the cows are sickly and well past their prime. In his embarrassment and anger, the father tells Nachiketa the equivalent of "Go to hell!" by saying, "I send you to Yama!" Yama is the God of Death, so Nachiketa, confused by the hypocrisy he perceives in life, decides to use his father's curse as an opportunity to speak directly with Death.

Arriving in the underworld, Nachiketa is told by Death's henchmen that he is out of town on a business trip and not expected for several days. Nachiketa declares his intention to wait for Yama's return and begins meditating to quiet his mind. For three days and nights, Nachiketa remains immersed in meditation and does not notice Yama's arrival. Yama inquires about the young boy sitting so intently at his entryway, and he is told by his assistants that they have never seen anyone approach Death with such grace and unwavering focus.

Yama is impressed with the young boy's discipline. Apologizing for making Nachiketa wait, the God of Death offers him reparations for his poor manners. When asked what he wants, Nachiketa first appeals for his father's forgiveness. Yama assures him that when his father learns that his son has safely returned from the clutches of Death, he will enthusiastically forgive him, as grievances often lose their importance in the face of loss.

This ancient myth highlights the essential importance of forgiveness. Forgiveness is a prerequisite for inner peace. Holding on to grievances, regrets and resentments is a certain recipe for perpetual suffering. Each of us needs to consciously decide if we are willing to relinquish our need to be right in the service of peace, harmony and love. Whenever two people disagree, both are convinced they are right and the other is wrong, justifying their antagonism and legitimizing their hostile actions.

Transforming judgment into understanding allows peace to replace hostility. Understanding fosters forgiveness, which dissolves anger and fertilizes hope. This is the foundation of emotional freedom.

Forgiveness brings divinity to humanity. More than a mere mood or sentiment, it radiates from a heart that has released pain, resentment, regret, disappointment and guilt. Forgiveness is a practice. It has the power to release constrictions in your heart that inhibit your ability to love.

Detoxify Your Heart

For thousands of years, Ayurveda has promoted an elegant program for physical detoxification. Known as *Panchakarma*, this three-step purification process includes preparation, elimination and rejuvenation. In the first step, toxins are loosened from tissues through herbalized oil massages and heat treatments. In the second step, toxins are flushed out of the system using potent cathartic herbs. In the final step, nourishing, easily digestible foods and herbs are ingested to rejuvenate and replenish.

An analogous approach can purify the human heart of retained toxic emotions. The first step requires loosening unhealthy feelings. In the second step, constricting emotions are released. In the third step, they are replaced with nourishing ones.

Try this process. Close your eyes, take a few deep breaths and tune into the feelings in your body. By now, I hope you are able to do this fairly easily. If you are experiencing sadness or disappointment, anger or regret, anxiety or confusion, allow yourself to experience your feelings, even though they may be uncomfortable. Using your breath, sink into the sensations, knowing that by allowing yourself to feel the discomfort, you are moving in the direction of releasing it.

Your emotions anchor the stories you tell yourself about love and life. As if watching a movie, observe those times when you were unable to meet your needs. See how the most recent emotional upset builds upon an earlier one. Allow yourself to follow the thread that ties your emotional history together. An abbreviated story might look like the following:

At Age . . .	This painful incident occurred . . .	I could not meet my need for . . .	I felt . . .
32	I Learned my spouse was having an affair.	Loyalty, devotion	Rage, despair

This reminds me of the time . . .

17	My high school sweetheart cheated on me.	Intimacy, trust	Anger, embarrassement

This reminds me of the time . . .

12	My father left my mother.	Safety, stability	Fear, bewilderment

This reminds me of the time . . .

6	My grandmother died.	Acceptance, security	Sadness, loneliness

Bringing emotions into conscious awareness is the first phase of emotional detoxification. In order to release something toxic, you must first identify what is constricting you.

To Be Without Sin, Cast the First Stone

The second phase is to consciously release the toxic feeling. Holding resentment and regret harms the person carrying the unresolved feelings much more than the perceived violator. The time, attention and energy consumed in vitality-depleting emotional ruminations are unavailable for life-affirming choices.

With the intention to release the toxic emotions, make a pilgrimage to a private location, preferably to a natural place, such as the ocean, a river or a mountain ridge. Bring with you a token object, such as a photo or memento, related to feelings you wish to release. Once at the site, gather together a pile of rocks in preparation for a ritual of emotional release.

Sitting quietly with eyes closed, bring your attention into your heart, envisioning the situation that generated the uncomfortable feelings from which you would like to be free. See if you can distill the experience down to a set of words or short phrases. For example, if you recently learned your partner has been having an affair, you might condense your thoughts and feelings to 1) a deep sense of betrayal, 2) embarrassment for ignoring obvious clues, and 3) guilt over sacrificing intimacy for financial security.

Using a marker, write each phrase on a separate rock. Hold the rock while bringing the images, thoughts and feelings encapsulated by the phrase into your awareness. Ask yourself,

"Am I ready to let go of this constriction?" If the answer is yes, focus your attention on releasing the congestion, and with the intention to let go, hurl the rock away from you. Shout from the depths of your being as you throw each rock. Swear, scream, shriek—allowing yourself to express the anguish and anger you have been carrying in your heart.

Continue identifying and releasing your accumulated hurts, disappointments and regrets until you feel spent and exhausted.

With each release, a wave of powerful emotions will rise to the surface. Allow your feelings to move up and out, without causing harm to you or anyone else.

Emotional Rejuvenation

Forgiveness is a powerful healing emotion. The next step in emotional detoxification is to replace the released painful emotions with nourishing ones.

Close your eyes, allow yourself to relax, and bring your attention into your heart. Feeling the subtle sensations of your heart, ask if you are ready to replace your regrets and grievances with forgiveness. If the answer is yes, ask yourself the following questions:

What would it require for me to forgive someone for the pain I have endured as a result of his or her choices?

What would it require for me to forgive myself for hurting another person as a result of my choices?

What would it require for me to forgive myself for hurting myself as a result of my choices?

When responding to these questions, it is important to recognize that we are asking what we can do, not what another person can do. We cannot control another person's thoughts, beliefs or feelings. We can express our feelings and request specific behaviors from another, but our forgiveness cannot be dependent upon a particular response.

When John's father unexpectedly died of a heart attack, he made arrangements to immediately return to his hometown. Although he had not been close to his family for years, he was unprepared for the hostility he faced from his older sister. She accused him of contributing to his father's broken heart by being unavailable to him. In addition to the loss of his father, John also felt deeply grieved by his sister's biting comments. He left shortly after the funeral, but his emotions festered, and John found himself having difficulties concentrating at work.

When he came to see me complaining of insomnia and fatigue, it was clear that John was beating up his father, his sister and himself over perceived sins of commission and omission. While he was undergoing physical detoxification, he agreed to pursue emotional purification.

Listening to his heart, John accessed numerous hurtful memories of times when his father did not meet his needs. Showing up intoxicated at his son's high school graduation, reneging on his offer to loan him money for a down payment on his house and leaving his mother for his office assistant were three of John's top grievances. In each case, his sister became their father's apologist, explaining away his broken commitments with defensive explanations. John perceived his father's sudden passing as his closing act of abandonment.

The cumulative effects of these disappointments resulted in a heart filled with feelings of sadness, anger and unworthiness. I asked John to write a letter to his father expressing his feelings around the various circumstances that had left their mark. After spending several days recapitulating his pain, he hiked to the Pacific Ocean shore and gathered up a pile of rocks. Over the course of two hours, he released his feelings into the ocean in a cathartic emotional discharge.

The next day, his mood was noticeably lighter. I encouraged him to write a story explaining his father's choices from a compassionate perspective. He took the next couple of days to piece together his understanding of his father's life. He chronicled what he knew about his father; that he was raised by alcoholic parents who divorced when he was seven years old; that his mother quickly remarried a cruel and jealous man; that his father's aspirations to go to pharmacy school were never fulfilled because he had to care for his sick mother.

As he recalled his father's disappointments and regrets, John felt sadness and compassion for the man for whom he had previously felt mostly disgust and anger. He was ready to forgive and move on with his life.

Commit to Forgive

The final step is performing an action that demonstrates your willingness to forgive the past so you can create a new future. Possible steps include making a phone call, writing a letter or paying a visit to someone with whom you have associated painful feelings. It may mean sending a letter to your former stepfather outlining the trespasses that occurred and expressing how his behavior caused emotional pain to you. It may mean calling up a former friend whom you hurt and apologizing for the pain you caused.

One of the most solemn holidays in Judaism is Yom Kippur, or the Day of Atonement. For twenty-four hours, adherent Jews fast and recapitulate their trespasses over the past year. Having acknowledged their human propensity to transgress, they renew their commitment to make choices that align with their core values. A beautiful expression says that for sins against God, the prayers spoken during the Yom Kippur service bring forgiveness, but for sins against another person, the prayers to God are not adequate. To clear the slate, a person must ask for forgiveness directly from the person they have harmed. This requires a willingness to be vulnerable and hear without defensiveness how one's choices impacted another's life.

Doing Your Best

Life is an evolutionary process, which means we are here to experience, learn and grow. If we cannot look back to earlier times in our lives without thinking, "If I only knew then what I know now," we would be wasting our time on earth. Expanded understanding of the consequences of our choices enables us to make better decisions.

A four-year-old who knocks over a milk carton while trying to pour herself a cup is doing her best. A sixteen-year-old new driver who gets into a fender bender is doing his best. A small business owner who makes a costly business mistake is doing his best. Although the consequences can be devastating, an unintentional trespass is usually easier to forgive than one in which we believe harm should have been avoided.

It's much more challenging to forgive when we believe that someone knowingly hurt another person. Lying, emotional or physical abuse, stealing, committing adultery, indulging in addictive behaviors—the pain and anger generated by these choices are more difficult to release because we ascribe intention to the behavior. However, the practice of forgiveness means remembering that everyone is doing their best given their personal history and emotional resources.

People are responsible for their actions. Forgiveness does not imply that we tolerate thieves stealing, teenagers lying or partners cheating. We can disagree with and not tolerate a behavior even while we understand the trespass in terms of immaturity, inability or limited awareness.

Each of us has succumbed to shortsighted, selfish interests that resulted in unpleasant ramifications. Understanding that, like you, other people are doing their best can help foster forgiveness and the freedom it brings.

Commit to Improve

If I have harmed you as the result of a past choice and seek your forgiveness, I must be willing to take responsibility for my actions and their consequences. In taking responsibility, I acknowledge that if I am presented with a similar situation now or in the future, I commit to making a different choice.

If you know that when you drink alcohol you become emotionally abusive, asking for forgiveness requires your commitment to get the help you need. If your teenager has been cited twice for speeding within the past three months, his request for forgiveness requires a commitment to safer driving. Forgiveness has healing and transformational power when accompanied by a commitment to live more consciously.

If you are having difficulty forgiving yourself for some misbehavior, make a commitment to perform some act of service that in some way compensates for your transgression. Volunteer at a local shelter, make a financial contribution to a charitable organization or give some spare change to the next homeless person on the corner. Consciously engage in intentional acts of service, and forgiveness will replace self-loathing.

Daily Forgiveness

Forgiveness is an essential component of a spiritual practice. I recommend you spend some time reviewing your day each night before going to sleep. Begin by practicing a mind-quieting meditation technique, either by using a mantra or following your breath for ten minutes. Then review your experiences from the time you awoke in the morning to the time you got into bed. As you play back your day's video on the screen of your awareness, notice if your body generates signals of discomfort, implying that something did not go exactly the way you wanted it to. Notice your response to the situation and see if your perspective can shift, based upon other information you become aware of or by recognizing that you may have been distracted or overloaded by other concerns at the time.

This exercise provides opportunities to practice forgiveness. Look at the pattern this behavior falls into, and see if you can gain some insight as to why you tend to respond this way. Then ask yourself what action you need to take to make things right and embrace the forgiveness you are seeking.

As you review your day, you recall a heated exchange between you and a coworker. Following up on a sales lead, you learned that someone else from your company had already contacted the customer. Feeling embarrassed and irritated, you confronted your colleague, accusing her of trying to steal your lead. She responded by saying that the customer had been forwarded to her extension. Upon realizing it was in your territory, she sent you an e-mail with the contact information. By the time you checked your e-mails and realized that you had inappropriately accused your associate, she had left for the day.

You now have an opportunity to practice forgiveness. Take a few minutes to calm your mind, and then review what happened. Identify the feelings that were generated as a result of your interpretation. Look at the pattern that this behavior falls into, and see if you can gain some insight as to why you tend to respond this way. Then ask yourself what action you need to take to make things right and embrace the forgiveness you are seeking. In this example, it might mean offering a sincere apology and inviting your colleague to lunch.

Forgive the Unforgivable

There will be times when there is no possibility of either giving forgiveness to or receiving it from another person. The person may no longer be reachable or have passed on. If this is the case, it is essential that you relinquish whatever resentments, regrets or disappointments you are holding, for no outside event will catalyze your release from the bondage of your constricting emotions.

If you have been withholding forgiveness for someone who caused pain to you, use a releasing ritual to clear your heart.

Then commit to engage only in relationships that are nourishing and do not subject you to the pattern of prior trespasses. If you have been hoping for forgiveness from someone you hurt, acknowledge that you were doing your best at the time, and commit to words and actions that are life-supporting rather than life-damaging. Life is too short to carry the burden of a heavy heart. It does not serve you or anyone else.

Lighten Up

An Egyptian myth holds that upon death a person's soul travels to a dimension where his or her life is reviewed. The essence of a person is taken before the god Anubis, who oversees a scale. On one pan of the scale is the feather of truth. Anubis then takes the astral heart of the recently deceased and weighs it in reference to the feather. If the heart is lighter than a feather, the person's soul is liberated. If, however, the heart is heavier than a feather because it is filled with regrets, grievances, hostility and remorse, the soul is sent back for recycling. The message of the myth is to lighten up.

Self-pity is just another disguise of self-importance. Holding on to gripes from the past depletes you of vitality and prevents you from enjoying the gifts that are available to you now. Free yourself through the power of forgiveness and compassion.

I demonstrate my commitment to forgiveness by:

1) Listening to my heart and using it to reveal the need for forgiveness.

2) Recapitulating my life on a daily basis and taking steps to clear resentments I may be accumulating.

3) Taking responsibility for my choices while not taking myself too seriously.

THE SEVENTH COMMITMENT:
I COMMIT TO LOVE

Thou shalt not commit adultery
Exodus 20:14

Your soul and my soul
Once sat together in the Beloved's womb
Playing footsie.
Your soul and my soul
Are very, very old
Friends.
Hafiz

The human heart yearns for love, for love expands our sense of self. Love is a celebration of unity and a rejoicing in our essential interconnectedness. It is the doorway to freedom from isolation and alienation.

Love is expressed differently at various stages of life. As infants, long before we could pronounce the word, love was mother. With the recognition of individuality comes a sense of separateness. Mother expanded us from "I" to "we," from "me" to "us," and from "mine" to "ours." Without her we were vulnerable, isolated and helpless. In her presence, hunger evaporated into fullness, anxiety dissolved into security, and discomfort transformed into relief. In the arms of mother, we went from feeling insignificant and irrelevant to important and essential. This is the power of love at every stage of life.

As young children, we transferred these feelings to objects that augmented our sense of self. Our favorite things—a satin blanket, a baby doll, a toy car, a teddy bear—enabled us to expand our ability to influence the environment. We felt love for the props we empowered because they made us feel bigger and more important. Like mother, these transitional objects helped us feel safer, less vulnerable and more potent in an immense, intimidating world.

As adolescents and teenagers, we fell in love with personalities. Connecting and identifying with a favorite teacher, a classmate, a television idol or a pop star, our constricted sense of self expanded. We loved the art teacher or rock singer because through them we felt larger than we did without them.

During this stage of life, we also received lessons in the pain that comes when our expanded sense of self, dependent upon another, deflates. As a teenage girl, you may have been elated when a popular boy asked you to a party, only to collapse into despair when he broke the date and invited another. As an adolescent boy, you may have felt on top of the world when included in a basketball game with your high school neighbors, but then rapidly felt empty when you discovered that you were not invited to play the next day.

As adults we continue the quest for the expansion of self through our positions, possessions and relationships. We love a job, a house or another person because through the attachment to the object of love our sense of self grows. Navigating adulthood requires developing the skills to balance the various spheres that expand our sense of self. Conflicts arise when one dimension into which we would like to expand competes with another, as, for example, when our love for travel competes with our job, or when our love for work competes with our family. Managed skillfully, our playground expands; managed unskillfully, our territorial freedom shrinks.

Make Love Consciously

Human beings live on many levels simultaneously. We are physical entities, navigating the forces of the material world. We are emotional beings, negotiating the world of identity. We are spiritual beings, exploring the unknown and the unknowable.

Love is expressed physically through affection and sexuality. Sexuality is propelled by the impulse for biological creativity, which may be the most powerful force in the world. While making love, the past is forgotten, the future is relinquished and the present moment becomes your totality. The boundary between self and nonself blurs as your mind quiets and you become attentive to the sensations, sounds, tastes and smells of the sexual experience.

Commit to make love consciously. When expressing love physically, allow your lovemaking to expand your sense of self as you explore the boundaries of where you end and your partner begins. Celebrate your powerful procreative (*pro creative*) energy, allowing it to bring you into present-moment awareness, where time and space lose their hold on you.

Sexual energy is potent, and like any powerful force, it has the potential to be used creatively or destructively. The commandment not to commit adultery recognizes that sex, by its very nature, is boundary expanding and can be boundary breaking. In most relationships, the power of sexuality reinforces intimacy within a commitment and weakens intimacy when there is not one. Crossing a sexual boundary in the context of a committed relationship is frequently accompanied by deception, which generates further emotional turbulence. To rationalize the behavior, unfaithful people often become increasingly critical of their partners, disturbing the peace of all involved.

Rather than viewing sexuality as a moral issue, see it as an opportunity to consciously direct your creative energy to connect intimately with another person. Sex is mostly fantasy. See if you can rekindle the passion in your primary relationship, nurturing freedom and peace, rather than conflict and turbulence. If, despite your best efforts to heal and transform a relationship, it continues to create misery for you and your partner, take a break and allow both parties to gain some clarity and perspective. Then make the choice you believe will provide the greatest likelihood of expanding peace, well-being and love in your life.

I Love You Because You Meet My Needs

When the mind is your internal reference, love is expressed through revelation—sharing your memories and dreams, thoughts and beliefs, fears and fantasies with those with

whom you feel safe. It is one of life's great paradoxes that w
invest so much energy in honing our self-image in the hop
that it will attract those who love us unconditionally. W
acquire positions of power and objects of status in our ques
to find people who love us despite our positions and posses
sions. We strive for fit bodies and fashionable clothing in ou
search for lovers who will see through our packaging.

Love between people is a contract to meet needs
Ultimately, it is a commitment that I will be there for you
when you are thriving *and* when you are struggling, and you
will be there for me. Love is a commitment to help those we
love heal their boundary rifts even as we embrace their
unboundedness.

Make the commitment to consciously communicate your
needs and hear the needs of your loved ones. This is the
highest expression of personal love. You are capable of creating more loving relationships by taking responsibility for
your feelings, identifying your needs, being willing to stay
vulnerable and asking for what you need, rather than expecting the people in your life to read your mind.

As children, we expect our caregivers to know what we
need and provide for us without having to ask. A wail or cry
may have been enough as an infant to get what you wanted,
but this is not the most effective approach as an adult.
Expanding upon the insightful work of psychologist
Marshall Rosenberg, I encourage you to practice conscious
communication in all your relationships.

1) Avoid the tendency to apply patterns from your past to the present situation.

The ancient part of the human mind is designed to fit current experiences into patterns based upon the past. In a hostile environment, it is generally better to overreact to a potential threat than to mistakenly assume no danger is present. However, behaviors useful in one environment may not be of value in another. Evolution rewards those capable of adapting to changing circumstances.

In modern life, emotional conflict is more likely to disturb one's peace than physical danger. Avoiding the tendency to immediately apply a label offers a passageway to emotional freedom.

When your partner leaves dishes in the sink or clothing on the floor, refrain from accusing him or her of "never cleaning up" or "always treating me like your maid." When your sister is late for a lunch date, avoid telling her that she "is hopelessly self-centered" or "never respectful of anyone else's time." Rather, express as accurately as possible what happened that upset you: dishes used at lunchtime remain unwashed in the sink; socks removed two days ago are under the bed; it's now 12:30 and your date was scheduled for noon. Staying present with what is happening empowers you to resolve the conflict more directly, without digging up accumulated resentments from the past.

2) Distinguish your feelings from your beliefs and interpretations.

Whenever you use the word "that" after the word "feel" you are most likely expressing a belief rather than a feeling, as in, "I feel *that* you don't appreciate me" or "I feel *that* you care more about the people at your office than you do about your family."

Become aware of the tendency to react to your interpretation of other people's intentions, as in, "I feel that you are taking advantage of me" or "I feel that you are taking me for granted." When you use language that expresses a sense of victimization, you paint yourself into an emotional corner from which the only way you can escape is if other people change their behavior. If you choose to feel "manipulated," "betrayed" or "neglected," you will not feel comfortable until the other person stops manipulating, betraying or neglecting you.

3) Embrace vulnerability as the means to meet your needs.

When describing emotions, people are often fearful of expressing the discomfort they feel. However, if you accept the premise that your feelings are your feelings, then the expression of emotions becomes a process of providing information to the people around you.

Practice describing your internal state using expressions like, "I feel sad, jealous and empty." Although these are not comfortable feelings to acknowledge, you are declaring ownership rather than holding someone else accountable. Notice the subtle but profound difference in the message when you say, "I feel insecure," versus "I feel you are neglecting me." In the first expression, you are providing information about your internal state. In the second, you are holding someone else accountable. Favor expressions that demonstrate your willingness to assume ownership for your feelings, rather than giving the responsibility to another.

4) Accept that it is your role to identify what you need that you are not getting.

Most upsets occur when people are not receiving the affection, attention, appreciation or acceptance they need. The clearer you can identify what you are missing, the easier it will be to communicate it.

Affection is expressed through loving touch. As mammals, our physiology is stabilized through touch. Touch helps lower blood pressure, enhances immune function and generates natural pain relievers. Nurturing physical contact instantly reduces anxiety and feelings of alienation.

Attention is expressed through eye contact. Most people are uncomfortable looking into another's eyes for more than a brief moment because it makes them feel vulnerable. When we make direct eye contact, we connect soul to soul. Making eye contact equalizes social hierarchy; therefore, most adults are usually uncomfortable with this level of intimacy. Young children, on the other hand, who have not yet developed the need to protect their self-image or status in society, crave direct eye contact, frequently inviting others to staring contests. If you want to give someone your attention, look them in the eyes.

Appreciation is expressed through words and actions that demonstrate the value others bring to your life. Telling and showing people that you appreciate them can have transformative effects on any relationship. Express how their behavior enhanced your life rather than resorting to pat labels. For example, if words of advice from a friend inspired you to take positive actions, express how they helped you, instead of saying, "You're so smart." Expressing your appreciation more consciously encourages greater intimacy based upon equality.

Acceptance is the natural expression of an inner dialogue in which unity predominates over differences. The more self-accepting you are for both your light and dark sides, the less judgmental you will be of those around you. If you find yourself vigorously reacting to minor qualities in other people, ask what this is telling you about yourself.

Every relationship can be a mirror if we are willing to look into it honestly. When we react disproportionately to another person, it is usually because they are mirroring back something we do not want to acknowledge in ourselves.

If what you perceive as your friend's flirtatiousness at parties really irritates you, it may be that a part of you would like, but is afraid, to be more outgoing. If you find yourself ruminating about someone in your organization whom you perceive to be power hungry, see if you can identify that aspect of your personality that would like more authority. Identifying and accepting the multiple facets in your nature will enable you to be more accepting of, and therefore more at peace with, those in your life.

Commit to being generous with your affection, attention, appreciation and acceptance, and you will see the same returned to you in kind. These expressions of human love will help fulfill your deepest intimacy needs.

5) Understand that how you communicate your needs is as important as what you say.

For most people, the left hemisphere of the brain is responsible for expressing and understanding the words of language. The right hemisphere is responsible for expressing and understanding the emotional content of language. Some psychologists estimate that only 20 percent of communication is in the words we speak, with the vast majority of information carried in tone of voice, facial expression and body language. The difference between sarcasm or sincerity, criticism or appreciation, and malice or compassion can be subtle. Be mindful of how you are expressing your needs through both what you say and how you say it. The more skillful you are in communication, the more likely you are to have the effect you seek.

6) Ask for what you need.

Get clear on what behaviors will meet your needs. Rather than insisting that your friend pay more attention to you, ask to go for a walk together after dinner. Rather than demanding that your partner be more affectionate, ask for a hug now. Rather than threatening that if your spouse does not stop spending so much money, you'll go bankrupt, ask to sit down and create a budget together. The more specifically you can express your need for a specific behavior, the more likely you are to have the need met.

A need communicated with an implied threat (*if you don't . . . , I'll . . .*), cultivates inequality in the relationship. Even if the person wants to give you what you are asking for, demanding it mobilizes resistance. Skillfully expressing your desires enables other people to feel better about themselves by meeting your needs. Relationships in which both parties trust that their needs will be met generate love. Become a master in conscious communication and you will become a master in lovemaking.

Sacred Love

It is easy to recognize that you have a body and a mind. Your soul, by its very nature, is not as easy to identify, as it is the observing part of you, silently witnessing your experiences and choices. As you are reading these words, see if you can identify these three layers: your body, your mind and the field of awareness that is awake and observing your thoughts and experiences.

When this witnessing aspect of your being becomes your

inner point of reference, it becomes easier to feel the commonality between you and those around you. The differences between your physical characteristics and beliefs become less important than the unifying principle of awareness that connects you. From a spiritual perspective the goal of love is to see yourself in the other and the other in you. This state of unity consciousness is the expression of divinity in humanity.

Most of us spend considerable effort honing our self-images through our positions and material possessions. Securing a good job and acquiring material abundance are worthy goals; yet we also know (or at least sense) that we are not our positions or possessions. As the layers of our self-image become more transparent, we recognize our underlying awareness—our spirit—as the essence of who we really are. When we recognize this within ourselves, it becomes easier to see through the disguises donned by others.

As long as the inner conversation of "I," "me," "my" and "mine" predominates in your thoughts, relationships will be seen as sources to fill your needs. As you become more self-reflective your sense of identity begins expanding. Rather than approaching experiences in terms of "What do I get out of this?" an expanding heart asks, "How can I contribute to your peace and well-being?"

When you feel centered, open and comfortable, the gates to your heart begin opening. Love thrives in an environment of safety, and there is no greater security than knowing that your essential nature is not dependent upon your accomplishments and acquisitions. You are worthy of love simply because you exist.

In sacred love, your loving becomes less like a laser beam and more like sunlight. Feeling comfortable within yourself, your inner contentment spontaneously helps those around you feel more comfortable. Your ability to connect with others supports more fulfilling relationships on all levels as your ego-based tendency for constant comparison and judgment quiets. As you become more open to seeing yourself as an expression of the sacred, you begin to see others in this same light. Knowing that the human experience is fraught with trials and tribulations, your compassion for others expands.

Compassion is the divine expression of love. Even as the uniqueness of individuality is honored and appreciated, a compassionate heart sees through the distinctions, embracing the unity. A heart filled with compassion is broadcasting the message, "I recognize you. I know you. I accept you."

Inner peace and security are the fruits of a compassion-centered life in which one's well-being is not dependent upon external experiences unfolding according to preconceived plans. A compassionate heart, tapping into the inner ocean of unconditional acceptance, flows in waves of love.

Love and Uncertainty

Your ego is continuously balancing risk versus reward. You can remain in a place of safety and security, but in doing so you relinquish the opportunity for expansion. You can take a risk to go beyond your usual boundaries, but this means moving outside your usual safety zone. The human heart is usually willing to take the chance, at times in opposition to the mind, which generally favors prudence over prospect.

Embracing the unknown provides our greatest opportunity for personal growth while provoking our greatest fears. Love and uncertainty walk hand in hand. Love takes us out of the mundane and the predictable into the magical and miraculous. When you fall in love, you become a different person. You may change your hairstyle, buy different clothing and listen to different music. Under the spell of love, you, who previously never danced, may find yourself enrolled in salsa classes. You, who never liked boats, find yourself enjoying a cruise around the bay. You, who hated classical music, find yourself going to the symphony. Love expands our sense of self, which, once expanded, never returns to its original size.

Expanding your internal reference point from ego to spirit allows you to surrender your need to control and instead accept what life has to offer. This inner dialogue of acceptance is the basis of a love-centered life, and a love-centered life is the basis of acceptance.

A life lived in love is the only life worth living. As expressed in 1 Corinthians, without love, knowledge and charity are empty. Between faith, hope and love, love is the greatest. Commit to love in all its expressions.

I demonstrate my commitment to love by:

1) Being generous with my attention, affection, appreciation and acceptance.

2) Practicing conscious communication in all my relationships.

3) Bringing silence into my awareness to expand my sense of self and capacity for compassion.

THE EIGHTH COMMITMENT:
I COMMIT TO ABUNDANCE

Thou shalt not steal.
Exodus 20:15

Even after all this time
The sun never says to the earth,
"You owe me."
Look what happens with a love like that,
It lights up the Whole Sky.
Hafiz

People on a spiritual path often struggle to reconcile the apparent contradiction between embracing wholeness and material abundance. Warnings about the spiritual risks inherent in the pursuit of abundance are present in most religious traditions. Christ told us it was easier for a camel to pass through the eye of a needle than for a rich man to get into heaven. In Buddhism and Hinduism, the monk's path of renunciation is promoted as superior to the ways of the householder. Knowing that in the end, we can't take it with us, why commit to abundance?

The answer is in the word. Abundance is derived from the Latin word *undare,* which means "rising in waves." The essence of abundance is the experience of the ocean of life rising in waves of love, energy and enthusiasm. If being spiritual means awareness of our connection to the creative source of the universe, we have the right to enjoy abundance in our lives.

Natural Abundance

Nature is inherently abundant. The universe is the ultimate expression of something coming from nothing, and the essence of the creation story is very similar whether you ascribe to Genesis, Vedic philosophy or quantum cosmology. From a biblical perspective, in the beginning God created light out of the timeless, spaceless void. From light he brought forth Heaven and Earth and then all things contained therein.

From the perspective of Vedic philosophy, creativity is an inherent quality of the universe. The universe as we know it is the expression of one exhalation of the Supreme Lord, Mahavishnu. When he inhales, the current cosmic manifestation will dissolve, until Mahavishnu's next breath when he recreates time and space.

From a modern scientific perspective, the known universe was born 13.7 billion years ago, when all that is perceivable was compressed into an infinitesimally small and dense point. This point erupted with a "Big Bang," creating energy, matter, time, space and causality. Whether the universe will continue expanding forever, or at some point begin collapsing, remains a point of debate.

Nature is intrinsically abundant. The number of named plant and animal species on earth exceeds 1.5 million, which is estimated to be less than 10 percent of the total that exists. Some biologists speculate that if we identified all the bugs and fungi around us, we could have 100 million carbon-based earthly neighbors. We are discovering approximately ten thousand new species each year, so it will take awhile to have a complete census.

Scientists have identified between four and five thousand bacterial species in a single gram of soil, while over 30 million worms can be found in a square meter of tropical grasslands. We share this planet with twenty thousand species of fish, almost 10,000 species of birds and a little more than three thousand species of mammals.

Mother Earth has shown her prolific creative capacity since life-forms first arose nearly 3.8 billion years ago. During the Cambrian explosion, a little more than 500 million years ago, biological evolution had a lovefest, generating more than 100 major animal groups, only about 30 of which survive to this day. During every epoch of the Jurassic period, when for 150 million years reptiles ruled the planet, it is estimated that approximately six thousand different types of dinosaurs were present. The complete tally of dinosaur species may eventually come in close to 20,000.

Moving from terrestrial to celestial, the known universe is currently estimated to hold (10^{21}) stars, which is a 1 with 21 zeros after it: 1,000,000,000,000,000,000,000. To further expand your mind, scientists now suspect that all the known matter and energy is only about 4 percent of what exists. The other 96 percent of the cosmos is currently believed to consist of dark energy and dark matter. In addition to unfathomable quantities of energy and matter, the universe is abundant in mystery.

Starving at a Banquet

The human species is early on the learning curve in accessing and distributing this abundance, with striking disparity in living standards between rich and poor countries. Annual global per capita income ranges from over $50,000 in Luxemburg to under $500 in East Timor. The world's three richest individuals are worth more than the combined wealth of the world's 48 poorest countries.

Over 1 billion people live on less than $1 per day; over 800 million world citizens receive inadequate nutrition. It is estimated that worldwide over 24,000 children die every day from starvation or preventable illnesses related to malnutrition.

These tragic facts reflect a poverty of will and creativity, not a lack of abundance. Fear-based choices consume valuable material and intellectual resources. Approximately $1 trillion of military spending will occur worldwide this year, with the United States accounting for more than 40 percent of the total. A recent United Nations report sadly identifies armed conflicts as the leading cause of hunger in the world. We have enough resources. We need to expand abundance consciousness.

Present Moment Abundance

Take a survey of what you have right now. Start by taking an inventory of your material possessions: your house, your car, your entertainment center, your furniture, your books, your jewelry and your bank accounts. Imagine packing up all your possessions into stacked boxes as if you were getting ready to move to a new home. Translate all your financial assets into either dollars or gold and include it in your packing. (Remember, the largest dollar denomination currently in circulation is a $100 bill.) Now ask yourself, how many more boxes would I need to feel I have enough?

The chances are that no specific, quantifiable goal will ensure peace or happiness. Over the years, I have known people worth billions who never have enough and many others with much less who live in a state of perpetual abundance.

I recently came across this illustrative story. A rich man was fishing next to his mansion on a lake, when a poor man, using only a stick and a string, sat down about fifty yards away. Within an hour, the poor man caught two fish and went home. This same scene was repeated day after day for two years, until finally, the rich man approached the poor man saying, "I've been watching you and considering your situation. If I were you, I'd fish a couple more hours each day and sell the additional fish in the marketplace. After six months, you could earn enough money to buy a small boat and new fishing equipment. Soon you could earn enough money to start a real business. Then you could hire other people to fish for you, and then you could do anything you wanted for as long as you wanted." The poor man thought about this for a moment and then replied, "To tell you the truth, sir, that is exactly how I am living my life now."

Abundance is a state of mind in which you believe you are intrinsically creative. You are inherently confident that your basic needs will be met. Your inner value is independent of your outer possessions. You recognize that the universe is abundant, and that you are an expression of the universe.

Commit to abundance consciousness. On a daily basis, before going to sleep, take an inventory of your life and allow your heart to fill with gratitude for the things, experiences and people in your life. Even during those times when your life is not unfolding the way you would like it to, bring abundance into your awareness, and you will notice a shift in your perspective. With this inner shift, you will observe a spontaneous decongestion in the external circumstances creating turbulence for you.

Abundantly Simple

The law of gravity tells us that objects of mass exert attractive forces over each other. As a baseball falls to earth, the planet rises ever so slightly to meet it. In a similar way, anything that you possess exerts ownership over you. The house, automobile or business you call your own requires you to serve it. Knowing how things that you own have the tendency to own you, choose your material possessions consciously.

Make the commitment to keep abundance flowing regularly by clearing unnecessary clutter from your personal space. Clean your car, especially the trunk and glove box. Go through your closets, drawers, attic, basement and garage, gathering up anything that you have not used for a while and are unlikely to use in the foreseeable future. Donate things that are not serving you to a local charity where they may add value to another's life. Give your extra stuff away to open the channels of circulation for abundance to flow.

A fifty-year-old gentleman came to see me from across the country, complaining of being physically and emotionally depleted. Although he had accumulated substantial wealth as an investment banker, he felt little zest for his life. His New York psychiatrist was recommending he go on antidepressant medications, but he wanted to see if there was a natural approach that could restore his enthusiasm for life.

In the course of my interview, I asked him the last time he remembered being really happy. He recalled that while working on his master's degree in business, he lived in a small condominium about half a mile from a state park. Several times a week, he would hike through the woods, which rejuvenated, centered and relaxed him. He felt at peace on his walks, regardless of the pressures at school.

Since completion of his MBA, he had been living in major

cities and rarely took time off. After getting married and having a child, the few vacations he took tended to be nearly as intense as his work. With his daughter about ready to graduate high school and go off to college, he was genuinely ready to rediscover himself.

It wasn't a difficult task. Financially, he was in a position to cut back on his work commitments if he was willing to balance what he wanted to do with what he had to do. I gave him a simple prescription: Take off a couple weeks and go someplace where he could hike in the woods.

He called me a month later to report that he had just returned from a trip to Oregon with his wife where they spent time in lush, old-growth forests. He had not watched television, checked his e-mails or taken a cell phone call for two weeks. He told me that not only was he feeling alive again, but a spark of passion had been rekindled in his marriage of twenty years.

He realized that his business success enabled him to engage in the simple things that brought him joy. For him, the commitment to abundance meant indulging in less rather than more.

One of my favorite stories is of a man who wanted to understand the relative benefits of material abundance versus the abundance that comes from a spiritual connection. He approached a wise teacher living in the woods who was known for his understanding of the ways of the world. The teacher agreed to address his question, but explained that the student's mind would be more receptive if he first learned to meditate. The teacher guided him into a deep meditative trance. He then asked him to bring him a glass of water before enlightening him on what he came to learn.

On the way to the well, the man encountered a beautiful woman, instantly falling in love. He courted her and soon thereafter, married her. When she became pregnant he started a business to support his family, and over time, became very successful. With his proceeds he expanded his enterprise, built a large estate and accumulated valuable art-work, sculptures and jewelry. Along with his financial success came influence, and soon he was considered one of the most prominent members of his community.

One day, while the man was on a business trip, a massive rainstorm moved in, overflowing the local river and flooding his home. The poor man lost everything: his home, his business, his valuables. In his deep despair, he wandered aimlessly through the woods, grieving his profound losses.

Suddenly, he found himself sitting in front of his teacher, who tenderly asked him, "Did you bring my glass of water?" The man realized that his entire experience of acquisition and loss and his accompanying enjoyment and desperation had taken place within his own mind. In this way, his teacher had given him the lesson in abundance.

Abundant in Purpose

If you had no concerns about accumulating things and had the financial freedom to do exactly what you wanted, what would you being doing now? This is the key question for those seeking abundance. Living in abundance consciousness requires looking deep into your heart and asking, "Why am I here?" If you believe, as I do, that everyone has a purpose in life, then discovering the reason for your incarnation is central to a life of abundance.

The expression of one's highest purpose in life is known as *dharma*. The seeds of cosmic intention have been planted in your soul, waiting to sprout when nurtured with self-awareness. As the bonds of a constricted ego-based identity are loosened, actions become increasingly aligned with universal law and one's highest purpose is revealed.

When you are doing what you are meant to do, no one could pay you enough to stop doing it. When your life is an expression of your deepest purpose, you are energized and enthusiastic because you are connected to the creative flow of the universe. Your actions bring fulfillment to you and add value to those influenced by your choices.

The commandment not to steal is naturally transformed into the commitment to abundance. The possibility of taking something from another without permission does not enter into your awareness, for based upon your experience, you trust that nature spontaneously provides for your needs.

You witness how people, attracted by your natural state of abundant consciousness, are inspired to support you in your life vision.

There are no spare parts in creation. Each of us is called to play our role impeccably, expressing the universal in our individuality. The challenge is to be awake so we can express the essential purpose of our life. When we are doing what we were made to do, we feel the flow of life moving through us and naturally serve ourselves, our relationships and creation.

The Power of Intention

There is a classical story about Arjuna, the archetypal human, training as an archer. The master instructor, Drona, assembled Arjuna and his brothers, placed a wooden bird in a tree as the target, and then asked the students to pull their arrows back on their bows, but not fire until given the command. Drona then went down the line of trainees asking each, "What do you see?" Each young man gave a similar response: "I see the bird and the tree, my brothers and my teacher," and each time Drona told the student to put down the bow without firing it. Arjuna was the last in line. When asked what he saw, he replied, "All I see is the eye of the bird." Drona asked if he did not see the tree, his brothers or his teacher standing by him. Arjuna replied, "All I see is the eye of the bird." Drona told him to fire the arrow, which he did, directly hitting the target.

This is the power of one-pointed intention. Successful people maintain an unwavering focus on the life they envision, while fully embracing each step of the journey. Even as inevitable obstacles arise, they are able to engage completely with the challenge at hand without losing sight of their ultimate goal. An intentional life is intrinsically abundant because the reward is in the journey, rather than the destination.

Intentions that arise from deep in your soul carry the power of destiny. It is the birthright of every person on earth to live a life of deep meaning and purpose. Because we fear that our children will not fit in as productive members of society, we compel them to find their niche, even if it does not allow them to express their unique talents. Then, as adults, we languish in jobs, even if we feel suffocated by the monotony.

You are not a cog in an industrial machine. You are a divine flame whose reason for being is to illuminate the world. If you are searching for your purpose, quiet your mind, bring your attention into your heart and ask yourself these questions. Then listen for the answers that come from the depths of your being.

What comes easily for me?
What God-given talent do I have?
What unique qualities characterize me?
What do I feel passionate about?
What do I do that gives rather than depletes me of life energy?

What brings me joy and enthusiasm?
What do I do that brings joy or value to others?
What do I engage in so that time loses its hold on me?

The checkout price for your life is everything you have accumulated. In the end, you will leave behind all your worldly belongings, your positions, your awards and your accomplishments. My belief, reinforced through my experience with many people at the end of their days, is that as we are preparing to exit, we are not taking an inventory of our material wealth. Rather, what brings peace in our final days is the love we created with those around us. A life lived with passion and purpose is a life of abundance.

Worthy of Abundance

Do you have an abundance capacity? I sometimes sense that people have a limit on abundance they believe they deserve. When they reach their threshold, they subconsciously begin restricting themselves so they do not violate their self-imposed limitations.

I recently saw a woman of modest roots who built a highly successful business with her husband. After building the company for over two decades, they decided to take the company public. On the very day of the initial public offering the woman was admitted to the hospital with her first bout of ulcerative colitis. Simultaneous with becoming a millionaire many times over, she was receiving intravenous fluids and tube feedings. For the next year she required steroids to control her digestive inflammation, which resulted in a weight gain of over thirty pounds. She came to see me seeking to improve her digestion, lose her accumulated weight and regain her energy. The timing of her illness with her financial success seemed too coincidental so I explored her story. She told me that as the oldest of five children, she was expected to be perfect, but she consistently disappointed her overwhelmed mother. On more occasions than she could remember, her mother told her that she was worthless and would never amount to much. Despite these predictions, she succeeded academically, married a terrific man and had a natural talent for managing people. Still, as the time approached for the company to take a major step of growth, she felt tremendous conflict over becoming wealthy, questioning whether she really deserved it.

Over several sessions, we worked on releasing the guilt that was inhibiting her from embracing the abundance. We also explored changing her self-sabotaging inner dialogue from how much she deserved to how she could allow more energy to flow through her. As she began to view herself as a conduit rather than as a reservoir, she became excited about the many ways she could use her money to benefit others as well as enjoy herself. Over the next year, she did a much better job of attending to her own needs, lost all her extra weight and experienced only minor short-lived exacerbations of her medical condition. She also made generous time and financial commitments to organizations dedicated to helping children with inflammatory bowel disease.

If you suspect that you are imposing limits on your own abundance because of a sense of unworthiness, shift your focus from what you want to possess to how you can express your energy and creativity in the world. The symbols of abundance—a bigger house, a new car, an ornate piece of jewelry—can brings waves of delight, but do not sacrifice the ocean for a few transient waves. Commit to a life overflowing with abundance of love, passion, creativity and meaning and the symbols will chase after you.

I demonstrate my commitment to abundance by:

1) Giving away things of value I have accumulated that are no longer serving me.

2) Regularly taking a gratitude inventory of what I currently have in my life that brings me joy.

3) Finding my passion and investing my time in those things that I love to do and do well in service to myself and those around me.

The Ninth Commitment:

I COMMIT TO TRUTH

Thou shalt not bear false witness
against thy neighbor.
Exodus 20:16

If you think that the Truth can be known from words,
If you think that the Sun and the Ocean
Can pass through that tiny opening
Called the mouth.
O someone should start laughing!
Someone should start wildly laughing—
Now!
Hafiz

Playwright, poet and first president of the Czech Republic Václav Havel once said, "Keep the company of those who seek the truth, and run from those who have found it." If you keep this in mind as you search for meaning and purpose in life, you will have a better chance of discovering truth while experiencing more joy and freedom in the process. Throughout the history of humanity, philosophers, sages and mystics in pursuit of truth have come to the same conclusion as Einstein, who maintained, "The search for truth is more precious than its possession."

Of course, history is replete with the stories of individuals and groups who believed they had found the truth and with it, the right and obligation to impose it upon others. From the Crusades to the Inquisition, from fascism to Maoism, those who believe they are in possession of the truth often destroy those reluctant to embrace their reality. At this very moment, there are eight "major" wars (defined by at least one thousand battlefield deaths per year) and approximately two dozen "lesser" conflicts occurring on the planet. The overwhelming majority of all wars are fought by people over religious, ideological or political beliefs.

There may be times and circumstances when it is justified to defend and even die for a belief, but sadly, our primitive patterns of reacting often result in violence as an early rather than last resort. Recognizing that most people confuse their strongly held beliefs with the truth, let's look at what it means to commit to truth.

Relatively True

People most commonly use the word truth to describe their core beliefs. Today on the radio, I heard the prime minister of France saying, "The truth is, the most important problem facing our country is high unemployment." This may be his honest belief, but I suspect there are many Frenchmen who might argue there are problems of higher priority. Political candidates regularly tout their truth about the health of the economy, the military and our social systems, but the nature of relative truth is that it changes with changing perspectives.

People beginning a statement with "the truth is" usually believe that what they are saying is self-evident and beyond argument. These are frequently the very expressions that generate the greatest resistance in others. Fervent certainty expresses what a speaker would like to believe is true, but often masks unspoken doubts. Thomas Mann, the German

Nobel Prize-winning author, once expressed the profound insight, "We are most likely to get angry and excited in our opposition to some idea when we ourselves are not quite certain of our own position, and are inwardly tempted to take the other side."

The commitment to truth begins with acknowledging that beliefs are inherently relative. The first Noble Truth of Buddhism's eightfold path is right perspective. This principle recognizes that everyone believes that his or her perspective is the right one. The pursuit of truth requires us to see that truth can wear many masks, each convinced that it is the one true face. If you can see that your perspective is one of many possible points of view, you are on the road to experiencing the truth that sets you free. According to Mann, "A great truth is a truth whose opposite is also a truth."

What do you believe is true? If you are a devout Christian, you believe that accepting Jesus Christ as your personal savior is the path to eternal life. To a Christian, the New Testament is the ultimate authority on truth. If you are a devout Jew, you believe that the one God, Hashem, made a covenant with Abraham, which was reinforced when Moses was given the Ten Commandments. To a Jew, the Torah is the ultimate authority on truth. If you are a devout Muslim, you believe that there is no God but Allah, and Mohammed is his prophet. To a Muslim, the Qur'an is the ultimate authority on truth.

If you are a scientist, you believe that there are laws of

nature that can be known through observation and interpretation. Although you may deny the existence of ultimate truth, Newton's laws of physics, Darwin's evolution and Einstein's relativity are the immutable principles through which you see the world.

Political truths, although often vigorously defended, are seldom as easily characterized. We need only look at today's world to recognize that truths, over which people fought and died during the last century, seem almost irrelevant now. Communist China and countries once part of the Soviet Union are today among the most fervent capitalistic nations, while most Western states have comprehensive socialized health care and retirement programs for their citizens. Ideas about truth change over time.

Creating Truth

Human beings have beliefs. Evolving human beings have evolving beliefs. For ideas to evolve, we must balance a commitment to core values with an attitude of flexibility and openness. This is not easy for most people, because although we may acknowledge the value of adaptability, our minds crave certainty.

Sigmund Freud once suggested that neurosis was the inability to tolerate ambivalence. Your human mind strives to classify ideas and experiences into neat categories. We see this frequently during political campaigns in which candidates are compelled to take a clear position on an issue or be accused of indecisiveness. Although initially the complexity of an issue may be acknowledged, once a point of view is taken, it is forcefully defended as the one true perspective.

It is helpful to understand the psychological process that leads to defining something as true. Whenever we come across a new concept, our mind registers the information and looks into our memory banks to see if we have encountered it before. We then make a determination as to whether or not we like the idea. Although we may try to convince ourselves that this is an intellectual exercise, it is actually determined emotionally, based upon whether or not we believe the net effect of the concept will bring comfort or discomfort to us. Often our feelings associated with an idea have more to do with whom we share the idea than the concept itself. If we believe that owning an idea will bring us increasing comfort, love, power, security or happiness, we declare ownership, at which point we say, "I believe this is true."

Deciding to own an idea implies your willingness to defend what you believe to be true. You may even believe it is justified to go on the offensive toward those who disagree with you. The desire to avoid the anxiety associated with ambivalence compels you to accept things as true, exclusive of anything that opposes it. Falling into the trap of constricted awareness may provide temporary relief but will eventually disturb your peace as other perspectives challenge the one you've chosen as true. The commitment to truth calls you to discover the point of view that is aligned with your core values while relinquishing your need to defend it. When you are deeply rooted in your own truth, you lose the need to convince others.

What Do You Hold to be True?

Take a few moments now to consider what you hold to be true about these complex issues facing humanity. Reflect on each one, noticing your initial position. Then see if you can acknowledge that under the surface, your perspective may be a little murkier than you might choose to admit.

Abortion
Animal rights
Assisted suicide
Cloning
Death penalty
Fossil fuel consumption
Genetically modified food
Global trade
Global warming
Nuclear power
Space exploration
Stem cell research
Terrorism
Undocumented immigration

You may notice that although you have an avowed point of view, you can recognize some ambiguity at a deeper level. You may notice that your position on one subject may put you in conflict with your position on another. For example, you may be vehemently opposed to nuclear power, while simultaneously having serious concerns about global warming. Although you may be a fervent animal rights activist, you may be conscientious about feeding your companion cat or dog the highest quality animal-based foods. You may be a strong supporter of stem cell research while feeling uncomfortable about applying genetic engineering to augment the global food supply. Although you may passionately believe in a woman's right to choose, you probably do not favor abortion as a method of birth control.

People invest considerable emotional energy in the defense of beliefs they hold to be true. Although this may seem obvious in regards to religious, political, economic and moral beliefs, I frequently see people fervently invest their emotional energy in dietary preferences (low fat versus low carb, vegetable versus meat-based) and health care approaches (allopathic versus naturopathic).

The commitment to truth requires you to continually review your beliefs about the world and your place in it, expanding your capacity to embrace multiple perspectives. As you become less rigid in your perceptions of truth, you become capable of respecting and empathizing with people of diverse beliefs. Maintaining your truth while remaining open to others' points of view has a healing and transformational effect on all relationships: personal, work, cultural and international.

Personal Truth

The most distressing internal conflicts that create anxiety and depression in people usually result from the inability to reconcile opposing truths. Like the old cartoons in which a character trying to make a choice has a little angel on one shoulder and a devil on the other, people create situations for themselves that seem irreconcilable. A woman I saw this week highlights the challenges that arise when truths collide.

Kathleen was in distress. A forty-year-old tax attorney, she was suffering with several migraines per week and had not slept well in over a year. She lamented that the communication with her husband had deteriorated dramatically over the past two years. Although Kathleen recognized that since beginning marriage counseling a few months ago he seemed to be making a genuine effort, she continued to feel resentful toward him and was poised to leave the marriage.

According to Kathleen, her husband had been so involved in his business that she felt neglected. She complained that the passion had gone out of their relationship, and she went numb whenever he tried to touch her. She acknowledged that he was a good father to their teenage sons, had never abused her and was not an alcoholic. When I asked if he had been faithful to her, she replied, "As far as I know."

The way she responded suggested there was something else under the surface, so I asked about her own fidelity. I could see her debating how she would respond. Finally after a long pause, she broke down and tearfully confided that she had been having an affair for over a year. She had not revealed this to her personal therapist, whom she had been working with for over nine months, or to her marriage counselor. Of course, she had been hiding this from her husband.

Without indulging in a discussion about the morality of extramarital affairs, we discussed how the lack of truthfulness was creating emotional and physical anguish for her and those around her. She realized that the only way to free herself from her intense distress was to get clear on what was true for her and align her words and actions with her true beliefs. In Kathleen's case, she needed to either proceed with a trial separation or relinquish the affair. She needed to find what was true for her so she could stop squandering her life energy.

The truth comes out eventually, because like trying to hold a beach ball under the water, it requires an enormous amount of psychological and physical energy to suppress it. Although it may be suppressed for a while, sooner or later it finds its way to the surface. Like a buried treasure in the desert, the sands of time ultimately reveal the truth that was hidden.

Your soul is in search of peace. Although the mind has an extraordinary capacity to rationalize almost anything, the more elaborate the rationalization, the more unsustainable turbulence is created. You may deny your alcoholism by justifying your drinking as a temporary response to stresses at work, but eventually this unstable situation will have to be addressed, such as your job stress being eliminated when you lose your job.

You may rationalize your embezzlement at work as acceptable because you are not being fairly compensated for your contribution, and therefore cannot sustain the lifestyle you deserve. At some point, the truth will emerge and a substantially simplified lifestyle will be imposed upon you.

You may rationalize your extramarital affair because your spouse is ignoring your needs, but the turbulence generated by the clash of powerful feelings affects all your relationships, directly or indirectly. The truth may not emerge until one has died; still, choices made in the past have ramifications.

It is a core principle of life that the universe creates the circumstances in which truth sees the light of day. The ninth commitment encourages you to make the choice to stay in alignment with truth whenever possible, while recognizing that you, like everyone else, is trying their best.

In Pursuit of Truth

Every thought you think and action you take has a consequence. The consequence of the thoughts in your mind is played out primarily through the molecules of your body. Turbulent thoughts create turbulent molecules, resulting in disruption of your body's peace, such as insomnia, indigestion, headaches or immune imbalances. The consequences of your words and actions are played out in the world. The words and actions you choose can contribute to peace and joy for yourself and others or can create turbulence and misery.

Why do people avoid facing the truth? We learned early in life that our actions sometimes elicited negative consequences. Breaking your mother's favorite vase, hitting a baseball through the window or going to a friend's party when your parents thought you were studying generated uncomfortable responses when the truth surfaced. After a few of these experiences in which you discovered there was a penalty for your actions, you made the calculation that denying the truth might save you from punishment. Although it usually only delayed it, the hope that you might dodge a bullet springs eternal.

From celebrities to heads of state, we see a familiar scenario played out. A trespass occurs; the trespass is discovered; the trespass is denied; apparently irrefutable evidence surfaces; the denial of the trespass generates greater consequences than the trespass itself. Still, we witness public events in which by denying the truth, a person appears to temporarily evade paying the price. Recent acquittals in high-profile cases are examples. But even though a jury may find someone innocent on the basis of a legal technicality, the loss of prestige and reputation (not to mention the civil suit awards) extracts a significant toll. On psychological and spiritual levels, commitment to truth is almost always the best choice.

Are there times when withholding or distorting the truth is evolutionary? Every person at some time has withheld the truth, distorted the truth or consciously lied. There are little lies and big lies. In the embracing of the uncertainty of truth, there will be situations when not telling the truth may be the best response at that time.

If a friend has confided in you something about which they feel vulnerable, it may be an expression of your higher self not to respond honestly when interrogated by the town gossip. If your spouse asks you how they look in a certain piece of clothing, being completely forthright with your opinion may not always serve the greater good. Not telling the truth may be the most evolutionary option when the truth can cause tremendous harm to others. If a tyrant wants information about the location of an intended innocent victim, withholding that truth is the right thing to do.

A spiritual warrior is skilled in timing and finesse. The commitment to truth is unwavering; knowing when to conceal and when to reveal it is key to a successful life.

Universal Truth

Is there such a thing as universal truth? Believing in the literal interpretation of sacred texts, fundamentalist theologians hold an unwavering belief in the absolutism of their "ism." Every true believer is certain that they have a monopoly on truth, and therefore, it is impossible for anyone outside their belief systems to be secure in their truth.

Universal truth would not be limited to a particular time or location. It would have no beginning and no ending, and it would be applicable across culture and history. Perhaps the closest we have come to a universal moral truth is the Golden Rule to "treat others as we would want to be treated." Variations of this principle can be found in all the spiritual and religious traditions of the world, either in the form of *doing to others what you would want done to you or not doing to others what you would not want done to you.* If humanity embraced both sides of this simple principle, we'd experience a lot less conflict in our personal, societal and international relationships. It reflects the basic belief that on a deep level we are alike and ultimately one.

Evaluate your choices in terms of whether the truth you embrace takes you in the direction of unity or separation. When evaluating which truth to own, consider whether a choice brings you increasing freedom and peace. Then make the choice that carries your sense of self from constricted to expanded.

The ninth commandment calls us not to bear false witness. A true witness is one whose awareness is in the present. A true witness does not encumber this moment with past judgments or ideas about how things should be. A true witness is able to separate present moment observations from past laden evaluations and future desired outcomes.

Your commitment to truth fulfills the intention of the ninth commandment: you acknowledge what is; you ensure that your perspective is aligned with your highest values; you embrace the fantastic complexity of life.

I demonstrate my commitment to truth by:

1) Noticing other points of view that may also be valid whenever I take a strong position on any issue. Practicing flexibility in my perspective on truth expands truth in my life.

2) Seeking opportunities to express my truth in ways that bring increasing freedom and joy to me and those affected by me. Using timing and finesse, I seek to maximize happiness and minimize suffering as a consequence of my thoughts, words and actions.

3) Making choices that move me in the direction of absolute truth by asking if my choice will help calm mental turbulence, expand my awareness and lead to peace.

THE TENTH COMMITMENT:

I COMMIT TO PEACE

Thou shalt not covet thy neighbor's house;
thou shalt not covet thy neighbor's wife,
nor his manservant, nor his maidservant,
nor his ox, nor his ass,
nor any thing that is thy neighbor's.
Exodus 20:17

For a day, for just one day,
Talk about that which disturbs no one
And brings some peace into your
Beautiful eyes.
Hafiz

Ask anyone, and they will tell you they want peace. The question each of us must answer is what we're prepared to do to attain it. Many of the world's tyrants justify their actions as necessary to achieve peace. Unfortunately, peace achieved through violence inevitably leaves its residue, so that sometime later, pain and resentment rise to the surface and the cycle of violence in the name of peace continues. The Tenth Commitment calls us to end this cycle.

The desire for peace is at the root of all other desires. Whenever we long for anything, we anticipate that our discontent or dissatisfaction will resolve once we achieve the object of our desire. When we feel constricted or incomplete, our minds seek things outside ourselves in the hope that adding something to our incompleteness will bring us peace of mind.

Our essential nature is peace, but with our individuation, we develop a sense of incompleteness. Our separation gives rise to desires: the impulses to move from less to more, from fragmentation to unity, from fear to peace. In the Jewish mystical tradition of Kabbalah, there is the beautiful concept of Tikkun, which means restoration. Divine light was originally held in ten crystal vessels, which were too delicate to contain the light. Seven of the ten shattered, leaving only Will, Wisdom and Understanding. The light from Justice, Loving-kindness, Beauty, Splendor, Power, Righteousness and the Spirit of God escaped. The purpose of each individual life is to contribute to the return of wholeness—to help repair the shattered vessels. In the process of restoration, peace returns.

Cosmic Hide-and-Seek

Life is a fantastic game of hide-and-seek with the Divine. Out of unity we create our individuality and then spend our lives seeking to reestablish our original wholeness. If you remember playing hide-and-seek as a child, you may recall that you had two competing fears. One was the fear of being discovered and one was the fear of not being discovered. If your hiding place was too well concealed, you may have intentionally made noises to attract attention so that you would not remain alone forever.

The desire for peace and the desire to stir things up is part of this cosmic game of hide-and-seek. If we were totally established in peace, we would not have an incentive to do anything. We would sink into inertia, and creativity would evaporate. Life is engaging because we are perpetually moving from peace into turbulence and then back again into peace.

Children demonstrate this propensity numerous times per day as they oscillate between contentment and distress. They can be sweet and happy until they pass by a candy store. Suddenly, a raging craving for jelly beans possesses them, and their peace is destroyed. If their parents submit to their ranting and buy them the object of their desire, within a few moments, they return to a state of lovable serenity (at least until the sugar kicks in).

The same process applies to adult human beings. Your car is running perfectly, but when you see that your neighbor has just purchased the latest model, the desire to buy a new automobile takes hold of you. Your peace is disturbed and you become convinced that the only way to restore it is to acquire a new car. You then embark on an energy-consuming ritual to fulfill your desire. First you read the reviews on the car and then research the options you must have. You explore the pricing, engage in negotiation and, finally, achieve ownership. Your peace is restored, and in a short time, your mental state is back to where it was before the desire took hold (at least until you notice the first scratch or receive your new insurance bill). Inevitably, there comes a time when your level of peace after buying the new automobile is the same as it was before the desire ever arose.

Desire is the basis of all pleasure in life. Listening to beautiful music, receiving a delightful massage, seeing a spectacular sunset, tasting a delicious ripe strawberry, inhaling the fragrance of a night-blooming jasmine—these sensory-rich experiences create impressions that generate memories that give rise to the desire to repeat the pleasure. We do not want or need to give up our desires to have peace. We need to establish ourselves in peace so every desire is experienced as a wave on the ocean of peace.

Envisioning Peace

Try this exercise. Close your eyes and take a few deep breaths. Now consider what is happening in your life. Ask yourself, "What am I striving to achieve? What do I want to resolve? What am I longing to acquire?" Notice that your endeavor to achieve, resolve or acquire usually arises from some sense of discontent. Now imagine that you are able to completely fulfill your desires. You have created the successful business. You are engaged to the love of your life. You have the dream house you've been working years to acquire.

How do you feel? Are you at peace as a result of fulfilling your desires? If the answer is yes, then see if you are able to envision that this inner state of contentment can be independent of situation, circumstances and events in the world. If you can imagine peace by projecting how you would feel as a result of reaching your goals, then your peace need not be held hostage to external symbols. This does not imply that you simply need to retreat to a cabin in the woods and wallow in peace. Rather, establishing peace as your internal reference enables you to access the energy and creativity that will support the fulfillment of your desires.

On the other hand, you may notice that even when you imagine owning the car you've always wanted, getting the job you've dreamed about or the relationship you've longed for, you still feel internal discontent. This is a common consequence of investing happiness in outer acquisitions or achievements, for like a child with a new toy, each wave of enjoyment rises and falls, inevitably giving rise to a new desire.

Each desire arises from a state of relative peace and, if fulfilled, eventually returns to it. Since almost every desire eventually takes you back to your original state, I encourage you to cultivate a state of inner peace that is not lost along the way. Being peace-centered enables you to enjoy the world without repeatedly losing yourself in the experience of loss and gain.

Peace in Action

In the Eighth Commitment, I mentioned Arjuna, the archery student with intense focus. Arjuna goes on to become the hero in one of India's greatest spiritual stories, the "Bhagavad Gita," or "Song of the Gods."

In this epic drama, a clan has become divided amongst itself and is about to go to war. Arjuna is the leader of the Pandavas, who represent integrity, freedom, love and peace. The opposing forces of treachery, selfishness, tyranny and conflict are embodied in the Kauavas, and their leader, Duryodhana.

Arjuna is torn by the conflict between his head, which tells him he must fight the war, and his heart, which feels love and compassion for his extended family on both sides of the battlefield. He engages in a conversation with the Divine represented by Lord Krishna, who takes Arjuna above the battlefield. Krishna helps him quiet his mind, so that he can see from a Divine perspective that life is a perpetual process of transformation in which everything is moving through some point in the cycle of birth and death. Krishna explains that the soul—the ever-present witness—is transcendent to this cycle of beginnings and endings. This state of nonduality is known as yoga. Arjuna is liberated by this shift in his perspective and logically comes to the conclusion that since peace is a state of awareness, no battle is required. Krishna, however, tells Arjuna that the fighting must take place to reestablish the forces of good and evil in the world.

He tells Arjuna that he must first go beyond the realm of duality—birth and death, right and wrong, good and evil—and then act in accordance with his highest values to establish peace and harmony in the world. The expression in Sanskrit is *yogastah kurukarmani*—established in a state of unity and peace, perform impeccable action.

The commitment to peace does not imply that you should withdraw from the challenges of life. It does not imply that you relinquish your intentions, goals or desires for abundance or achievement. It does mean that you should make developing an inner state of peace your highest priority.

When peace becomes your practice, you will find yourself in a perpetual state of gratitude for every life experience.

Mind/Body Peace

Your mind and body are inseparably woven together. Anything that disturbs your mental peace simultaneously creates a disturbance in your body. Similarly, imbalances in your body inevitably disturb your peace of mind. Notice that if you had an argument with your spouse this morning, you may still be experiencing uncomfortable sensations in your body. Notice that if you overate at lunch today, your physical indigestion generates turbulence in your mind.

Hundreds of scientific studies have confirmed that mental peace is good for your health while mental turmoil is bad. For example, psychologists have identified that an important independent risk factor for a premature heart attack is hostility. You are probably familiar with the standard risk factors for coronary artery disease—hypertension, elevated cholesterol, smoking and inadequate physical exercise—but in large studies there was always a certain proportion of people who had normal blood pressure and cholesterol levels, never smoked and exercised regularly. When evaluated from a psychological perspective, an emotional pattern emerged. People who scored the highest on tests designed to measure hostility: 1) felt other people were untrustworthy, deceitful and selfish; 2) frequently experienced the emotions of irritability, impatience and loathing; and 3) considered anger and aggression as acceptable ways of responding to the world. Those who had the highest hostility scores had the greatest risk for heart attacks.

Long-term studies of medical doctors found that hostility put physicians at a six-time higher risk for dying prematurely compared to those who learned to take life a little easier. The angriest lawyers also have a much higher risk of premature heart attacks than their more peaceful colleagues. In a recent Boston study, hostility was a more important contributor to heart disease than high blood pressure, smoking and high cholesterol levels.

Other research has shown that a turbulent mind weakens one's immunity. A Harvard study measured immune function in people watching violent battle scene images and compared them to others watching Mother Teresa comforting children in her orphanage. Images of violence have an immune-weakening effect, whereas images of compassion are immune-strengthening.

Hostility is harmful to your body, mind and soul. See how many of the following statements apply to you.

☐ I carry more than my fair share in my work and home relationships.

☐ Minor mishaps create a lot of frustration for me.

☐ Those who criticize me often have more faults than I do.

☐ It often seems that just as I'm ready to achieve a goal, the people I count on let me down.

☐ The times I have something important to do for myself is the time people around me want my undivided attention.

☐ When I can't find something, it's usually because someone decided to clean up and put it away without telling me.

☐ I find customers who spend time chatting with a store clerk to be inconsiderate and self-centered.

☐ People need to hear directly when their actions have negative consequences, even if their feelings are bruised.

☐ I feel annoyed when someone takes the seat in front of me at a movie.

☐ Frustrating situations often remind me of similar aggravating events from my past.

If you checked three or more boxes, you can benefit from some peace practice. For any statement that you identified with, consider how you might reframe your attitude from hostility to peace. For example, if you believe that most people around you are not carrying their fair share, begin noticing what other people are doing during the course of a day. Pay attention to how many things your partner, spouse or workmate manages during a day. By shifting your awareness from what you're not receiving to noticing what you are, the impulse to feel angry about how much you're doing may not arise.

If you have the tendency to feel irritated whenever someone engages in pleasantries with a clerk, make it your practice for one day to hold a pleasant conversation with every cashier you encounter. Ask them how their day is going or how long they have been working at the store, and notice how your irritability spontaneously subsides.

The next time you're ready to unload on somebody, take a brisk walk outside and do some deep breathing, grunting and groaning with each exhalation. Once you've blown off some steam, consider how you might express your concern in a manner that surprises rather than demoralizes the other person and notice if you get what you want and feel better about it.

Our world, with its festering wounds inflicted by millennia of conflict, is calling for a new response. If human beings are to participate in the next wave of evolution, we must overcome our ingrained biological and tribal reactions and explore new methods of resolving conflict. We cannot relinquish this responsibility to our political leaders, for they simply represent our collective awareness. Our collective consciousness reflects the totality of individual awareness. How each of us thinks, speaks and behaves in our small universes contributes to the ways of the world. The Tenth Commitment calls you to demonstrate your willingness to choose peace over hostility.

Seven Peace Principles

Acts of peace and violence have ramifications in the world. Thoughts of peace and violence have ramifications within our bodies.

Our primate biology is not clearly wired to choose peace. Although we used to imagine that our closest genetic relative, the chimpanzee, with whom we share over 96 percent of the same DNA, was an innately peaceful being, we have since come to learn that chimps have a disturbing propensity to violence. Beginning in the mid-1970s we began observing violent battles between chimpanzee groups with occasional murders, and there are now numerous documented incidents of chimpanzee infanticide and cannibalism.

We can accept this biological tendency and rationalize that we are simply not designed for peace, or we can make the commitment to nurture the evolutionary possibility that selects for peace. Jonas Salk, the discoverer of the polio vaccine, once said that if human beings are to survive as a species, we must evolve beyond survival of the fittest to "survival of the wisest." He suggested that the next important phase of human evolution is *metabiological,* which means that rather than getting better at killing all other potential competitors, we find more creative solutions to nurture complexity and diversity on earth. Rather than thinking in terms of survival of the fittest, we should think about the survival of what best fits.

In support of this shift in evolutionary thinking, consider these seven peace principles. Bringing your attention to these principles will help you tap into the creativity that supports inspired evolutionary choices.

1. Peace is a state of being.

If you commit to peace, you will want your thoughts, words and actions to resonate with peace. Unfortunately, you will not be able to accomplish this unless your being is established in peace. The most direct and consistent way that I know to bring peace into every aspect of your individuality is through the regular practice of meditation. Take time on a daily basis to quiet your mind and calm your body. This helps you take peace beyond a mood you are trying to maintain to your essential state of being.

2. Peace is independent of what is happening around you.

You cannot wait for your circumstances to become peaceful before committing to peace. Inner peace is not dependent upon everyone around you being gentle, kind and compassionate. Although these circumstances would make it easy for most people to be at peace, the peace that passes understanding must arise from within. Access peace through your meditation practice and then radiate peace to your environment through your words and actions.

3. Peace is contagious.

Emerson said, "Who you are speaks so loudly I can't hear what you're saying." When I talk about peace in workshops and seminars, I'm often asked, "What can I do to get my _____ to be involved with this?" The blank is typically filled in with the words spouse, children, boss or neighbor. My response is that there is usually nothing you can do to get anyone to do anything. But if, as a result of this information, you are better able to radiate peace, harmony and love to the people in your life, you'll have a better chance of them asking you what they can do to have more of what you seem to have. Share your peace innocently and authentically and people will catch it.

4. Peace is dynamic.

Peace on a beach in Hawaii or at an old-growth hot springs is great, but we need a peace that is sustainable at the O'Hare airport, on a subway train in New York City or while driving in Los Angeles traffic. Peace at rest is one aspect; peace in action is another. Commit to peace in all its expressions. When your thoughts, words and actions are in alignment with peace, you are implementing the Tenth Commitment.

5. Peace is courageous.

Not resorting to violence is one of the most courageous acts a person can perform. The great peacemakers of our modern time, Mahatma Gandhi, Martin Luther King Jr. and Nelson Mandela, demonstrated the enormous courage that is required to be a peacemaker. Teach your children how powerful they are when they choose peace over violence. Reward them generously when they do.

6. Peace is not defined by its opposition.

The mentality of war requires there to be a clear separation between us and them, friend and foe, good and evil, right and wrong. Peace seeks unity. Those willing to commit to peace do not make enemies of those who seek aggressive means to their ends. They attempt to reduce the need for aggression. If force must be mobilized as a last resort, it is with the intention of neutralizing the aggression and creating the conditions for peace.

7. Peace is a practice.

Our primitive, biological nature is territorial, survival oriented and tribal. Our sacred, divine nature is generous, compassionate and forgiving. In any given day, most people touch both ends of their human spectrum. The commitment to peace does not expect that you will never get irritated, never raise your voice, or never say or do something you later regret. It does expect you to learn from your experiences and not make the exact same mistake repeatedly. Each night before going to sleep, recapitulate your day and see if through any words or actions you failed to express peace. If you identify some event that you believe could have been handled better, make the commitment to contribute to peace tomorrow.

Be loving and peaceful with yourself and you'll be better able to express peace to the people in your life. As a consequence, you'll find yourself judging, worrying and controlling less, while laughing, loving and enjoying more.

I demonstrate my commitment to peace by:

1) Noticing my desires as they arise and envisioning how I will feel once I realize my desires. I will remain centered and peaceful even as I strive to fulfill my wants and needs.

2) Identifying when I am demonstrating qualities of hostility and looking for ways to reframe my hostile perspective. I will seek ways to express my needs without damaging the people around me.

3) More consciously choosing to express peace in my thoughts, words and actions. As I prepare to go to sleep, I will review my words and actions, and see if I added to peace today. If I recognize that in my need to defend my self-importance, I contributed to turbulence in some way, I will make a commitment to contribute to peace tomorrow.

CONCLUSION
A COMMITMENT TO CELEBRATE

Now, sweet one,
Be wise.
Cast all your votes for Dancing!
Hafiz

I care about the future of our planet, and I care about the future of my three children. Max, who is twenty-four, now works with me at the Chopra Center, running our lifestyle division. Sara, eight, and Isabel, four, are providing me with a profound opportunity to consciously observe people becoming who they are. My beloved wife, Pam, is an amazingly consistent reinforcer of the values we hold and wish to impart to our children. It is not an easy task.

It's fully understandable to me why for thousands of years society has taken the viewpoint that the way to get people to do what they should is to threaten them with punishment if they do not. We used to use this tact regularly with our daughters—"If you don't get into your car seat now, you're not going to Legoland." "If you do not clean up the playroom now, you're not going to Build-a-Bear."

The problem with this approach is that it usually doesn't work, and even if it temporarily does, the price paid is rarely worth it. Instead, what we are finding effective is turning required tasks into play. Rather than forcing our kids to do what we want, we try to get them to want to do what needs to be done. We've started a game at our house called Simon 9-1-1 where whenever one of the girls makes a mess, someone shouts Simon 9-1-1 and we go into a frenzied cleanup to see how fast we can all put everything away. We set up races to see who can be strapped into their car seats first. We inspire them to eat foods with all the colors (red peppers, orange carrots, yellow peaches, green zucchini, blue berries, purple plums) so we need to nag them less about eating their fruits and vegetables. We are committed to reducing their commandments while encouraging them to make commitments they can honor.

It's time for us to treat each other this way. I know it's a dangerous world. I know that some people will commit crimes unless there is the threat of incarceration. I know that some people would drive dangerously if not for the threat of a traffic ticket. I also know that most people who behave badly came from environments where commandments ruled. Children treated badly often develop into resentful, defiant adults. If they do not act out in the world, they act out against themselves through addictive behaviors, poor health habits or failed relationships.

I envision a world where the threat of punishment is not

the primary motivator of good choices. I envision a society where people are encouraged to ask themselves the most important questions about who they are, why they are here and how they can best serve. I trust in the wisdom of the soul, which wants each of us to embrace the mystery of life, find our place in the universe and dance in celebration for having been invited to the party.

Start with one commitment—perhaps the one that seems the easiest for you. Commit for a day. If you are able to honor it for one day, see if you can commit for a week, then a month. You'll know a commitment has found a home within you when you no longer have to consciously tell yourself to honor it because you are already doing so. Once you've mastered one, choose another.

Make your commitments with a sense of curiosity and wonder. See what happens when you put your attention on the demonstration points for a day. Signs to look for may include:

- Being pleasantly surprised
- Getting what you want through unexpected channels
- Fretting less about the past
- Worrying less about the future
- Feeling more connected
- Laughing more
- Having more enthusiasm
- Losing unwanted habits
- Noticing more creativity
- Receiving more love

It is my personal experience and deep belief that commitment is more powerful than commandment. Individuals, families and communities living on the basis of commitment to their highest values do not depend upon external forces to keep the peace. Their choices are based upon the belief that worthy acts are those that reduce pain and suffering and enhance the peace and happiness of all sentient beings.

My hope is that when enough of us think, feel, speak and behave in ways that reflect a dedication to commitment not commandment, we will speed the evolution toward a better planet for the benefit of our children, grandchildren and generations to follow.

Ten Commitments
Workshops

Ten Commitments one-day and weekend workshops are held at the Chopra Center for Wellbeing in San Diego, California; the Chopra Center & Spa at Dream in New York City; the Rocky Mountain Chopra Center & Spa in Westminster, Colorado; and other venues throughout the United States. To learn more about Ten Commitments and other Chopra Center workshops, seminars and retreats developed by David Simon and Deepak Chopra, please call 888.424.6772, e-mail us at: *TC@chopra.com* or visit *www. chopra.com/tencommitments.*

For more information on

The Ten Commitments

workshops and other programs

with Dr. David Simon

please send an e-mail to

tencommitments@chopra.com

or visit

www.chopra.com

or call

(888)424-6772